Fifty States, Fifty Weeks

Fifty States, Fifty Weeks

☙

Exploring America with Family and Faith

George Arredondo

Copyright © 2015 George Arredondo
All rights reserved.

ISBN: 069236496X
ISBN 13: 9780692364963
Library of Congress Control Number: 2015913961
GMGG Management, Inc., Whittier, CA

This book is dedicated to my wife, Melinda, who has had the kindness and decency not to realize she's way out of my league.

And to my sons, Garon and Gavin, for teaching me to be a father first and to be a coach second!
And to my father, Felix, and mother, Bertha, for all the sacrifices they made to make our lives better. And to my seven brothers and sisters, David, Yolanda, Sandra, Patricia, Lisa, Alex, and Sylvia, whom I love deeply and I thank God for every day.

CHAPTER 1

The Long Way Home

IN LATE OCTOBER, my family and I were having lunch on an unbelievably warm fall day in Cape Cod in Massachusetts. We'd just discovered what most of America would know in a few days and would occupy the serious attention of people living in the Northeast: Hurricane Sandy, one of the deadliest and most destructive hurricanes in American history, a category-three storm spanning over one thousand miles, was heading right for us. How had I—a city kid from Los Angeles, over 3,030 miles from home, with the most important persons in my life—managed to drive a small, twenty-four-foot RV into the eye of one of the biggest storms of the century? For the first time in my life, I was scared. Correct that: really terrified!

Just a few months earlier, I had been the second-in-command at a company in Northern California with several hundred million dollars in annual sales, heading up a team of over a thousand employees, making great money, living in an affluent area with my wife and two sons. How had I gotten here from there?

It all started with a question: "If I had one year to live, how would I live it?" This question started me thinking about how I wanted to spend the rest of my life. Did I want to spend my next year, in Northern California, four hundred miles from my hometown and family? I knew the answer—and it scared me because that question threatened everything I'd worked so hard to achieve.

I'd been with my present employer nearly fifteen years and had worked my way up to top management, with the promise that I'd run the company when the current president retired. A graduate of the University of Southern California, I'd recently completed a yearlong MBA-type leadership program at the Harvard University Business School in Boston.

I was also one of the few college sports officials who worked at the highest level in two sports. I had an amazing run working with the Pacific-12 Conference in basketball and the Mountain West Conference in football. A prolonged absence would end my officiating career at the highest level, with many more games to officiate.

My family lived in a handsome home in an exclusive suburb, and my sons attended one of the best schools in the state of California. Thanks to a healthy salary and solid investments, my net worth had reached seven figures. My wife and sons loved our community, had many friends, and looked forward to continuing our present lifestyle for years to come.

How, I asked myself, could I even think about leaving a lucrative job and asking my wife and kids to move back to our native Southern California while I regrouped and figured out my next move? The truth was I couldn't ask them to give up everything they loved without offering an enticing and exciting alternative.

That was when it came to me: We'd take the long way home. Instead of driving four hundred miles south to Whittier, California, where my wife and I had grown up and still owned a smaller home, we'd head north, then east, then south, and then west and travel through all fifty states until we reached our destination—fifty weeks later.

The more I entertained the idea of visiting every state in the Union, the more excited I became—and I knew I needed to sell myself on the concept before I could get my family members to buy into it. I also realized I had to think through the logistics before I sold the greatest idea I'd ever had because I was sure that my wife, Melinda, and gifted sons, Garon, twelve, and Gavin, nine, would barrage me with questions.

The most glaring question was could we afford to do this? Much of our net worth was tied up in real estate, and we'd put away a good start for our retirement. However, what if we used the money now, when we were young enough to do something adventurous and the boys were willing to accompany us on the journey? After all, I was still in my forties, with plenty of work years ahead of me when we returned from the trip.

The notion of prolonged travel—fifty states in fifty weeks—was in some ways an unusual choice as a "next step" in our lives, since I'd spent the previous fifteen years traveling on business and away from home several days a week. However, I didn't equate business travel with a long-term journey—the former was hectic and draining, but I believed the latter would offer time for family bonding and cultural enrichment.

The primary consideration for an extended trip was my sons' education. How could I take them out of a highly ranked school and try to educate them at home—in an RV, no less? What if they were behind their peers when they entered classes the following school year? What if this affected their future prospects? What if they blamed me for ruining their lives?

Yes, this was the most difficult-to-face aspect of the fifty-states-in-fifty-weeks plan—how would it affect my sons? The second most daunting thought was, how would the trip affect my relationship with my wife? Would the togetherness create a stronger bond or cause us to drive each other crazy?

Lower on the list, but still something that floated through my mind, was how other people would react when they heard what I'd done. He what? Quit a great job, threw his family in a tin can, and drove around the country for a year? What happened to George? Did he go down the wrong road?

However, despite all these thoughts, trepidations, misgivings, and concerns, I realized one important fact: I had to commit to making this vision a reality. The commitment started with getting my family on board. It was June, the boys were about to get out of school, and I'd figured out a perfect segue. I could just ask, "What do you want to do this summer?"

That night, as Melinda and I were getting ready for bed, I posed the question. Here, let me interject that my wife feels most comfortable in a fine hotel that offers all the amenities, and she's not someone who gets excited at the prospect of roughing it. I can't say that I blame her. I mean, who doesn't enjoy clean, comfortable accommodations? Therefore, when I asked her what she'd like to do, I anticipated that she'd suggest Hawaii or another low-key, relaxing spot. Melinda might have had a hint that something was up, because instead of answering, she asked, "What do you want to do?"

At the outset, I want to say that I have the world's most spectacular wife—a wonderful partner, friend, and confidante. So often over the years, she has facilitated my dreams, ambitions, and brainstorms. I may come up with the ideas, but, in large part, she's the one who makes it all happen.

When Melinda turned the tables and asked what I wanted to do, she gave me the perfect opportunity to share my vision. As I explained what I had in mind—to preretire and spend all our time together as a family while visiting every state—she listened but didn't say much before falling asleep.

The next morning, when I suggested that we have a family meeting, discuss the trip with the boys, and set up a time to go look at RVs, she said, "It sounds like you're serious about this."

"I've never been more serious about anything," I told her.

"You have lots of ideas, George," she said. "And you're enthusiastic about all of them."

She had a point. I was always thinking of things for us to do as a family, things that were fun, exciting, enriching, creative, and dynamic. We had recently taken a week-long trip in a rented RV and enjoyed the flexibility and comfort of a house on wheels.

Now that she was wide awake, I let my enthusiasm move into overdrive, expressing how we could really get to know the country, learn how our nation was formed, and find out about the people who made this country great. I mentioned how the boys would love attending games at ballparks around the country and how we could explore the national parks and presidential libraries, experience regional cuisine, visit museums, tour historic sites, and share our love of this country with our sons.

After my impassioned appeal, Melinda told me, "George, I love living in your dreams."

One down and two to go.

That night, we held a family meeting and explained what we had in mind, visiting fifty states in fifty weeks. The boys had questions—lots and lots of questions. What about school? What about their friends? Why?

Again, I shifted into high gear and painted a picture of life on the road, telling them that this would be a once-in-a-lifetime, enriching experience, something they'd remember forever.

While it was important that my sons shared my enthusiasm for the journey and saw it as an adventure, as a parent, I felt that the decision resided with my wife and me. If we felt the trip was the best choice for the family, then the boys would have to respect our wishes and make the most of the opportunity.

Fortunately, we were able to address most of the boys' concerns, and soon they were poring over atlases to anticipate possible routes. We scheduled visits to RV dealers for that weekend.

The next step was to talk to my company's president and develop an exit strategy. However, when I explained that I intended to resign and return to the city of Los Angeles, my words didn't seem to register with him. Finally, he said, "Most people would think you are crazy, but I know your strong commitment to your family".

I didn't feel compelled to share the details of what I had in mind, so I only offered my sincere gratitude for the opportunity and my appreciation for all the business lessons learned.

During my fifteen years with the company, this man, whom I respected for his business acumen, had rarely taken time off or vacation and prided himself on his dedication to business. The problem was that he didn't want anyone else in his employ to take a vacation. If you tried, he usually manufactured an emergency that required you to turn around from wherever you were and head back to work. Many of his managers rarely took vacations due to guilt and pressure to be around in case of crisis. What was the point of offering vacation when players on the team did not take it? We recorded a record number of saved vacation hours, but this was not the point. It was the lack of healthy leaders with balanced lives. In fear of repercussions, they all fell victim to collecting vacation money and working non-stop.

I kicked myself for buying into this insanity for so long. People needed to take vacation and time off to rediscover and energize themselves. People needed to spend time with their families. People needed to unwind, relax, and reflect. After fifteen years without an uninterrupted vacation, I was about to take an extended journey—accountable only to my family, my faith, and myself.

I offered all the notice he required to replace me so I could turn over the reins to whomever my employer promoted into my position. However, if the corporate world fears one thing, it's someone labeled a "malcontent," an individual with the strength to say, "I can do better." The last thing a corporation wants is for you to stick around and contaminate other corporate soldiers with your malaise. Within days, I was ushered to the door—and there was no turning back. I was a free man. I had awakened from the corporate coma, the suspended animation I'd existed in for many years.

CHAPTER 2

Revving Up

As we prepared for our yearlong journey to all fifty states, I thought back to history class in elementary school, where we learned about the pioneers who'd headed west during the mid-eighteen hundreds. Yes, the pioneers had a rough go of it—and I used them as a measuring stick whenever I started to think that our trip might be too daunting. I'd stop myself and think, *If the pioneers could do it in a covered wagon, we can make the trip in an RV.*

We had a mountain of tasks to complete before we could leave—starting with terminating our house's lease. We were lucky. The owner was going to sell after our lease expired. We could check that off the list. Now we had to figure out what we needed to sell, give away, or put in storage. You can imagine the sorting, prepping, and yard sales; the trips to Goodwill; and the posts on Craigslist. It was exhausting, but we did it. We were able to close the door on our old life. Not that there weren't some twinges over leaving our community and our friends, but it helps when you're not just moving to a different location but embarking on an exciting adventure.

I tried my best to stay in the "George the Explorer" mode and get my family revved up about the trip. I also tried to take on as much of the planning as possible so that Melinda could focus on the most significant decision related to the trip: which homeschooling program to choose for our sons. Since Melinda was taking on the responsibility of homeschooling, it was only fair for her to select the materials she considered most appropriate.

Melinda spent weeks researching various programs and ended up choosing materials issued by a Christian organization. Faith plays a central role in our family life, and the fact that the materials had been approved by a Christian organization enhanced our confidence level about the choice.

My major form of preparation for the trip was reading. I always say that if you're thinking about doing something, find someone who has done it before. In the case of traveling around the country in an RV, I found a Kindle book called *How Not to RV* that proved invaluable. The main takeaways from the book were: don't over plan the trip, and do remain open to happenstance, chance, and God's plan.

Just as I'd compared our family to the pioneers—if they could do it, so could we—I figured if an individual who'd never traveled outside Manhattan could make it around the country alone in a used RV, I could certainly do it with my family in a new RV.

Reading stories of people who'd made the trip boosted my confidence, and I came to understand that building confidence and maintaining a positive attitude were the best ways to prepare for the trip.

At first, I wondered if we'd be able to accomplish all our preparations in just six weeks, but six weeks proved plenty of time to get ready. In fact, it might have been a bit too long to prepare, giving us excess time to second-guess our decision.

However, once we purchased the thirty-foot RV, we were committed. That's when the trip became real, with our RV, the modern version of the covered wagon with horse power. Only this wagon had all the comforts of home—including air conditioning and heat.

Now we just had to load it up, and load it up we did, cramming it full of clothes, cooking utensils, and other everyday necessities. We stuffed in as many books as we could; in fact, books were the number-one take-along item: hardcovers, paperbacks, audiobooks, and e-books. We were outfitted with a diverse library that emphasized the nature of the trip: history, the United States, and US presidents.

From Jennifer Flower's memoir *How Not to RV*, I'd learned not to over plan, so I tried to resist mapping out the entire route while waiting to hit the road. Actually "don't over plan" turned out to be the best piece of advice related to the trip—leading us off the beaten path and fostering an attitude of exploration and discovery.

I had decided to make my older son, Garon, who'd turn thirteen in September, my copilot during the trip, so I spent time with him before our departure, teaching him how to read maps, how to operate a GPS, and how to Google for directions. I was happy and excited, thinking that I'd have an entire year of full-time togetherness with my sons, creating the kind of childhood for them that I hadn't experienced and fostering the type of close relationship with them that I'd never had with my own father, even though I'd lived with him for a few years after my parents got divorced.

When my younger brother and I became too much for my mother to handle, she sent us to live with my father. I was thirteen at the time and needed direction, so my mother's decision was good from that standpoint. However, since my father was a workaholic and an alcoholic, living with him turned out to be more of a lesson about living on my own, since my father was really only home one day a week, on Sunday.

Part of the reason for making the trip around the country was to create wonderful experiences and beautiful memories for my sons—both things I hadn't experienced during my childhood. My father's only rule for my brother and me was to come home every night. We ran on the rough streets of Los Angeles and got into more than our share of scrapes and trouble, and I can say with no exaggeration that I am lucky to be alive.

I realized that my older son, Garon, was about the same age as I was when I went to live with my father full time. Perhaps it was some kind of unconscious desire to bring balance into my past that caused me to decide that my son would live full time—and this meant 24-7—with me for an entire year. Dad would be right by his side, and his brother's side, for fifty weeks.

Before the trip, I decided to help Garon put together a travel kit of personal-care items. As we picked out soap, shampoo, a toothbrush, floss, mouthwash, nail clippers, deodorant, and other items at Target, I asked myself, *who taught me how to do this?* I realized that I'd had to figure out most things for myself, and I hadn't always done the best job of it.

I survived a difficult childhood for one reason: my older brother, David. When I was a young teen, David was already in law school at UCLA. At least once a week, he would stop by our home, knowing my father wouldn't be there, and take my younger brother and me somewhere and spend time mentoring us. Sometimes we went to a basketball game, sometimes out to dinner, sometimes out for ice cream. It didn't matter where we went; my brother's care and attention were enough. I can never repay him for all he did for my brother and me. Now I wanted to make sure I was there in the same way for Garon and Gavin.

As we put together Garon's travel kit, I told him that someday he would teach his younger brother, and eventually his own children, how to do the same thing. While we moved from aisle to aisle in the store, I told him about my brother David and about how he acted as a hero to me.

It had been a long time since our family had visited with David's family—we'd lived in Northern California for over five years. I vowed to change that. As soon as the trip ended and we moved back to Whittier, I would make it a point to spend time with my seven brothers and sisters and my mother, who was now in her seventies. My father had passed away over ten years before, but somehow his influence lingered—mainly in what I decided not to do, starting with drinking, which I'd stopped doing in my early twenties.

As we toured the personal-care items in the store, I looked at the disposable razors and wondered if I should purchase some for Garon's travel kit. By the time we finished our journey, he'd be almost fourteen. However, I decided that could wait. I wasn't in a hurry for him to grow up but would be there for him when he did.

The timing of our exit from our home made it necessary for us to spend our last few days in a local motel. Our RV was ready to rock 'n' roll—decked out with Wi-Fi, computers, GPS, food, clothing, books, cooking utensils, accessories, personal-care travel kits, and just about anything else you can name.

Fifty States, Fifty Weeks

Each of us had something that was hardest to leave. For me, it was my job, which still occupied massive real estate in my thoughts. I kept thinking about all the years I had devoted to the company and how things could have turned out better. I was still trying to come to terms with much of it. For Melinda, the hardest thing to give up was her routine, a comfortable, predictable lifestyle. For Garon, the most difficult thing to give up was his Scout troop, where he thrived and had many friends. For Gavin, the biggest challenge was leaving his beloved Aunt Donna, who for many years had lived nearby and cared for him often.

However, despite all that we were leaving behind, we had each other and were growing closer by the day, reversing a long-standing trend of growing in the opposite direction. Years of working long hours and spending days each week on the road had led to breakdowns in communication and closeness with my wife and sons. It hit me that if I'd stayed in my job, it might have spelled the breakdown of my marriage and estrangement from my sons. More and more, I was realizing that fifty states in fifty weeks was more than just a fun family frolic—it was a way to redeem my family life.

Spending our final days in Northern California in a motel turned out to be a good thing—for one, the RV would feel like an improvement. For another, we already felt as if we were traveling, as if we had hit the road.

CHAPTER 3

Beginner's Luck

AFTER SIX WEEKS of planning and anticipation, the day finally arrived, August 1, when the Arredondo family would embark on its fifty-states-in-fifty-weeks adventure. We were excited and eager to get on the road, and we had selected Sacramento as our point of departure.

After snapping a photo at the facility where we'd stored our RV for the previous two weeks, we headed for the California capital. As soon as we got rolling, Gavin asked if we could pay one last visit to his favorite Target store in Roseville. My wife said she'd like to pick up some last-minute supplies—even though the RV was fully loaded. I thought the visit to Target would serve as a way for Gavin to say farewell to the place he'd lived for most of his life, so I agreed to make the stop.

While my wife and sons were in Target, I decided to let the RV run in order to test the cooling system, and I got out of the vehicle to stretch my legs before the first round of driving. As I stood there, I reflected on leaving our old life and riding into the unknown. Again, I reminded myself how brave the pioneers had been to leave everything and face so many hardships. Compared to what they'd gone through, our trip would be easy.

This California day was a scorcher, so I decided to get back in the RV and wait for Melinda and the boys to come back. However, when I pulled on the door, it wouldn't open. The keys were in the ignition, and my cell phone was on the driver's seat.

Just then, I saw my wife and kids exiting Target and approaching the RV. When they got within ten feet of me, Gavin shouted out, "You locked yourself out, didn't you?" When I nodded, they all started laughing. Here we were, fifteen minutes into our trip, not even at our first stop, and we'd been sidelined. In this case, the pioneers had it better—at least covered wagons didn't have locks.

Melinda called the AAA motor club, and while we waited, curiosity seekers approached, asking us where we were going and whether anything was wrong. I answered the first question and remained vague about the second question—offering only that we were waiting to say goodbye to some friends.

After about five minutes, I remembered something I'd learned in the one-day RV class I'd taken a few weeks before. The instructor had advised us to always leave a window unlocked—and I figured I'd followed his instructions. Sure enough, when I pressed on one of the side windows, it opened, creating a ten-inch gap I figured might be large enough for a nine-year-old to squeeze through.

While Melinda, Garon, and I were threading a willing Gavin through the window, we saw flashing lights. I turned to see a state police car behind us. Were we about to be arrested for breaking into our own RV? I rattled off our story to the officer, and I guess the tale was so outrageous that it had to be true because he moved on without even checking my license.

A triumphant Gavin let us back into the RV, and we were ready to get on with the trip. I tried to put a positive spin on what had just happened, saying, "If that's the worst thing that can happen to us, we're in good shape." A few hours later, I would realize I'd spoken too soon—way too soon.

As we drove to Sacramento, my family continued to tease me about getting us locked out. I laughed along, but my feelings were definitely mixed. I'd set myself up as the captain of the ship, the brave and wise leader who was going to navigate through the highways and byways of all fifty states, and here I'd messed up when we were just a few minutes into our trip. How was this going to affect the way my wife and sons viewed me? What would it do to their confidence level, their feelings of trust? I decided not to say anything and let them enjoy the humor of the situation until it blew over—after all, I'd never make that mistake again.

The area in front of the Sacramento capitol building is emblazoned with "No Parking" signs. We didn't intend to park—we just planned to stop for a minute to get a family portrait at the starting point of our journey.

As soon as we got out of the RV, we were lucky enough to encounter a passerby who offered to snap our photo. No sooner had we captured the perfect shot, with the capitol building in the background, then we again encountered the state police…but this time the officer wasn't as understanding, telling us to move it. Couldn't we read the signs?

We were off, heading north on Highway 5. After driving for a few hours, we pulled over and had lunch. One of the great things about RV travel is that you can stop just about anytime, anywhere, which gives you a real sense of freedom.

Back on the road, we were ready to make it through the next few hundred miles to reach the RV camp near the Oregon border, the only stop I'd planned.

However, about half an hour later, signs on the highway informed us that, due to a fire, the road was closed, starting with a particular exit. I asked Melinda to check whether the closure occurred before or after our destination, and she replied "before." So now what would we do? What else could go wrong?

Five minutes later, I found out. A huge diesel truck, barreling down the road at eighty miles per hour, flew past me, and what happened next seemed to take place in slow motion. With fire and smoke in the distance, I saw what looked like a metal pipe, about three feet long and four inches around, fly off the truck and into our lane.

I flashed back to the one-day RV class, where the instructor had advised that if an obstacle was in our path, we should drive through it rather than swerve and risk hitting another vehicle. Therefore, I drove straight ahead, and the next thing I knew, the RV was rocking from side to side. It was all I could do to keep the thirty-footer from tipping over.

Melinda screamed, and I guess the boys were too stunned to speak. I hung on to the steering wheel, trying to keep the RV on the road, the violent shaking accompanied by a loud banging sound under the vehicle. As we rocked, rolled, and banged, the fire raged ahead of us. Somehow, I managed to get to the right-hand lane and pull off on an exit.

After I stopped on the side of the road, I turned and asked, "Is everybody OK?" Melinda and the boys nodded, and all three seemed to take a deep breath in unison.

I felt shaky but proud that I'd navigated the accident well enough to bring my family to safety. I did my best not to let on how scared I'd felt and tried to minimize what had just happened. I stopped myself from saying, "We're lucky to be alive," and spent a few minutes reassuring my wife and sons that everything was OK.

To survey the damage, I hopped out of the RV to take a look under the vehicle—not that I had the know-how to figure out what was wrong. I knew next to nothing about the undercarriages of motor vehicles but did my best to scrutinize everything for any obvious damage, and nothing jumped out at me. I figured the banging sound was just the pipe hitting the RV as it bounced under it—no harm done. Relieved, I jumped back into the RV, told the family that everything appeared to be OK, and took the next ramp onto the highway.

As soon as we gained speed, I knew something was seriously wrong. The steering was tight, and it was all I could do to keep the RV headed in a straight line. Just then, I looked up and saw a sign looming from the side of the road: "Camping World." At the time, I considered this a stroke of luck—if your RV needs a repair, it doesn't hurt if the accident happens near a repair shop.

When I parked, Melinda and Gavin decided to stay in the RV while Garon and I talked to the people inside Camping World. We walked in around four thirty, feeling great that we'd made it there before closing time at five o'clock. As we entered, the staff members were standing around, chatting, leading me to believe they'd have time to take care of us—I mean, what else were they doing?

In a minute, the manager burst that bubble, informing us that they were booked up and couldn't even look at our RV for three weeks. I had to fight the urge to yell and tried to remain calm, mainly to provide a good example to my son.

Here was this manager, standing around, doing little, and he refused to even look at my vehicle. I told him I was traveling to all fifty states, was going to write a book about the experience, and did he wanted to come off as unhelpful and uncooperative in the story.

He replied, I could take the RV down the road to Robert's RV Repair Shop, where they might look at it. Then he reminded me that it was peak season for RV travel. All the repair shops were booked to capacity, and he doubted that anyone in the area would be able to help us.

Before we left, Garon turned to the Camping World manager and said, "My dad is a great speaker. He will write that book, and you're going to be in it for the wrong reason."

Camping World is a chain business, they like many in business forget who the customer is (and we needed help!) and I vowed not to stop at any of its locations during the trip—and I never did.

Just a few miles down the road, Robert's RV Repair Shop was the complete opposite. The place was a hive of activity, with RVs up on racks and service technicians bustling to take care of customers. Still, Robert himself took time to listen to what had happened to us and remarked, "That's an amazing story." He explained that he was extremely busy but would send someone out to look at our vehicle within thirty minutes. In the meantime, he plugged in our vehicle so we could turn on our air conditioning without running down our power.

Five minutes later, Robert came out to our RV along with an assistant. After looking under the RV for a few minutes, Robert stepped up to me and said, "Your muffler was sheared off, and your drive shaft is seriously bent. You're lucky to be alive." Well, someone had finally uttered those dire words—I was only glad he'd voiced them outside the earshot of my wife and kids.

Robert explained that this type of repair required a specialist and recommended another local mechanic. Everybody was closing up soon, but Robert said we could stay overnight in his parking lot. He would let us plug in, and he'd leave the door open to his shop so we could use his restroom. While we had a restroom on the RV, we only wanted to use it for emergencies because it required someone (namely me) to clean it out, and the captain preferred to avoid extra duty whenever he could.

The next morning, before we left, I tried to pay Robert for all of his consideration and assistance, but he refused to accept any compensation. This was a lesson I learned repeatedly: good people all over the country go out of their way to help.

At the next repair shop, we found out that it would take about two weeks to repair the drive shaft because they had to order the parts from the manufacturer. Two weeks? In Redding, California? I didn't want to spend two hours here. We were scheduled to fly to Alaska on August 15 and still needed to make our way to Seattle, where we were going to catch our flight.

The mechanic told us we could try to drive the RV the way it was, but we wouldn't get very far. He said he'd try to repair the damaged drive shaft, and if he could do so, we'd probably get back on the road within two days.

We had no choice and decided to make the best of it, renting a car and checking into a motel. After hearing our story, both establishments gave us their lowest rates. However, what could we do for the next two weeks—or if we were lucky, two days—in Redding?

Well, it turned out this wonderful community had lots to do and enjoy, including walking across the Sundial Bridge, one of the top pedestrian bridges in the United States, and visiting a local zoo. The citizens of Redding were friendly and helpful, and we enjoyed some of the best meals of the trip at area restaurants.

The first few days of our journey were filled with ups and downs, twists and turns, but luck is all in how you look at it. In two days, we were back on the road, heading north. The fire was over, the highway was open, and we were ready to find out what was around the next bend.

One of the key takeaways for me was that it's fine to plan, but if the plans don't work out, you have to adapt, remain flexible, and just experience the experience. Additionally, every day is a good day to realize that you're lucky to be alive.

CHAPTER 4

Not a Vacation—This Is Work

On August 3, we headed to Emigrant Lake, a large reservoir in southwest Oregon that serves as the centerpiece of a vast recreation area. It is a popular vacation spot, thanks to its beautiful location, which is surrounded by mountains and forests, and its water-related activities, including swimming, hiking, boating, canoeing, and fishing.

As soon as we arrived in the Beaver State, we gathered around the door of our RV, and Gavin had the honor of placing the Oregon sticker on our map of the United States, making it two states down and forty-eight to go.

When we stepped out of the RV, it seemed as if the trip were just getting started. This was how I'd envisioned fifty states in fifty weeks: visiting awesome places that offered an array of outdoor family activities.

Sunny and a perfect eighty-five degrees during the daytime, the weather was fantastic as we dove into everything the area had to offer. The boys especially enjoyed the three-hundred-foot water slide. Melinda, who found time to work out each day, appreciated running in such a gorgeous setting, and we all loved riding the bike trails and basking in the lake. I thought it was a nice bit of serendipity that the lake was named "Emigrant," because the Arredondo family was "emigrating" from its native California to visit every state in the nation.

George Arredondo

Now that we were enjoying fun outdoor activities and surrounded by hundreds of vacationers, we, of course, felt as if we were on vacation—even more so because the boys weren't scheduled to start homeschooling for another few weeks.

Everything seemed easy; all we had to do was park the RV, hook it up, and enjoy the surroundings. I allowed myself to drift into mental coasting, in which I began to think the entire trip would be a version of this kind of vacation-like fun, only in different parts of the country. It would take a shock to my system the following day before I straightened out my thinking and realized that the trip was not a vacation. It was our job for the next fifty weeks.

The wake-up call occurred on Highway 1 as we made our way up the Oregon coast. I can't point out one scary moment because the drive was dangerous and daunting from beginning to end. It was a bad time to realize that I'd purchased the wrong RV. The thirty-footer was just too big to maneuver with any ease, and here we were on one of the most treacherous roads in the United States. However, at the same time, it is one of the most beautiful.

As I did my best to navigate the sharp twists and hairpin turns on the two-lane road situated on narrow cliffs above the Pacific Ocean, I didn't have time to be scared. I was too busy watching the road and trying to avoid toppling over whenever a truck heading in the opposite direction passed too close and pulled the RV into the southbound lane for a near collision. The only good news was that since we were headed north, we were on the inside lane, away from the steep drop-offs to the ocean.

Highway 1, up the Oregon coast, is a difficult drive for a car, so you can imagine how it was for a novice RV driver in a hard-to-handle vehicle. I tried to stay cheerful and make Melinda and the boys feel safe and confident, but Positive George only got so far. I mean, who wouldn't feel frightened when thick fog rolls in and you can't see the white line on the road or the vehicles coming in your direction and doubt whether the other drivers can see you?

A few hours on this road felt like years, especially for Melinda and Gavin, seated in the back, where the vehicle shook and fishtailed. Every few minutes, Melinda pleaded, "Slow down," but whenever I did, the drivers behind me started to honk nonstop or tried to pass our RV, increasing the danger for all of us. I had no choice but to keep up a steady rate of speed, to Melinda's dismay. Sorry, Mel.

If I had been driving a car or had been a more experienced RV driver, I might have been able to revel in the majestic beauty of my surroundings. However, I had a job to do: get my family home safely after fifty weeks on the road. That was my number-one occupation. Yes, the trip was a job, not a vacation. I could never allow myself to forget it, even for a minute.

We saw a sign for Wildlife Safari in Winston, Oregon, and took the exit to get relief from the road and to explore this unique park. After driving east for ninety minutes, we ended up at the open-air zoo that features nearly six hundred animals from around the world, including tigers, lions, elephants, giraffes, zebras, and bears. The park rangers instructed us to keep our windows closed at all times, and we were more than happy to comply.

From the brochure we received at the entrance, we learned that Wildlife Safari is the brainchild of Frank Hart, who started the park to help save rare and endangered species from around the world. We really felt as if we were caravanning in the wild and even pulled over and made sandwiches while watching the animals outside the closed windows of our camper.

After parking at a nearby RV campground for the night, the next day we headed back to the coast and ended up in a quaint fishing port called Newport. In Newport, we had some of the best meals of our trip—including the boys' first experience eating fish-and-chips, which they enjoyed so much we returned to the restaurant two days in a row. The area features the Yaquina Head Lighthouse, a picturesque ninety-three-foot white tower completed in 1873 and still in operation, and the Oregon Coast Aquarium, once home to the orca that starred in the movie *Free Willy*.

Newport also offered a unique adventure for Garon and Gavin: crabbing, where they lowered a large metal basket into the ocean and, a short time later, pulled it out of the water to reveal a catch of Dungeness crabs. (Newport, Oregon, calls itself the Dungeness-crab capital of the world.) The boys' haul served as dinner for the evening—delicious!

Fifty States, Fifty Weeks

These last two stops, Wildlife Safari and the village of Newport, were filled with tourists and vacationers, but I tried to stay focused on the trip as work. The two days in Newport gave me time to stop and reflect on what was, for me, the biggest challenge of the trip: driving the RV. I grew up watching Jackie Gleason on *The Honeymooners* TV sitcom and now had much greater appreciation for Ralph Kramden's complaints about the difficulty of driving a bus. I can say without exaggeration that learning to drive the RV in a skillful, safe, and confident manner was one of the most significant accomplishments of my life.

On August 8, we drove about three hundred miles from Newport, Oregon, to Seattle, Washington, the Evergreen State, where we spent the night in an RV park. The next morning, we drove to the airport, parked our RV, and hopped on our flight to Anchorage, about a three-and-a-half-hour trip. We'd packed plenty of warm clothing, anticipating cold weather, at least during the nights.

After arriving in Anchorage, we took a taxi to the RV-rental facility and drove off in a twenty-four-foot C-class RV. After stopping at a supermarket for supplies, we made our way to Denali National Park, about 250 miles northwest of Anchorage.

During the drive, we kept pulling over at rest stops to take in the magnificent views of the mountains, glaciers, and big, big sky. When we stopped at the RV resort in Cantwell, adjacent to the national park, we were ready for a good night's sleep. While the boys dropped off right after a quick dinner of peanut-butter sandwiches, Melinda and I found it hard to fall asleep. At ten o'clock at night, it was still light outside. We tried taping dark T-shirts to the windows, but the sun still seeped through.

Lying awake, we had time to talk—well, whisper, so we didn't wake up Garon and Gavin—about what was, for us, a fascinating topic of discussion: our rental RV. We were flabbergasted at how well the RV handled and what a smooth ride it offered. It was a dramatic improvement over our RV parked back in Seattle. I had sort of a sick, sinking feeling when I realized that a vehicle more appropriate to our needs was available. I was too tired to think much more about this at that moment but knew

I'd have to give it more thought soon, very soon. It was part of my job to make sure we were in what was, for us, the best RV in terms of safety and comfort.

The next morning, August 10, Melinda and I both felt tired and had gotten little, if any, sleep, but the kids were well rested and raring to go. After having cereal for breakfast, we hiked to a nearby lake, and the boys made a bridge from stones, which Melinda tried to cross but didn't quite make it.

After our hike, we packed up and set out for Denali, a national park that encompasses more than six-million acres and is home to Mount McKinley, the highest peak in North America, a mountain that the indigenous people called "Denali," meaning "great one."

We'd arrived late in the season for Alaska, and few fellow travelers were on the road or at the RV site. I counted only three RVs in a park with room for fifty. We later learned that most people visit Denali on a tour bus—not in an RV.

As we traveled through Denali, I was awestruck at the pristine frontier. This was how the original settlers had seen America: unspoiled, untouched, intact, with no telephone poles, electrical wires, or strip malls anywhere in sight.

As we learned later in the trip, most of the people we encountered during our travels said that Alaska was the top place they'd like to visit. I'd felt the same way, and now I was here, with my family. I'll say, for the record, that Alaska should be on everyone's bucket list as a place to visit at least once—and you don't have to stay in an RV because nearby hotels have buses to take you through the park.

While I reveled in the majestic surroundings, I had to stay in work mode, especially now that we were so isolated, making us vulnerable in a variety of ways. We could have a breakdown, encounter an angry mother bear, or be held up by roaming thieves. I tried not to characterize this as worry and preferred to think I was acting with caution.

I'd read in a book that it was a good idea to have walkie-talkies in the wilderness, so I'd ordered some online before leaving on the trip. If the boys rode their bikes, even a short distance, they had to take a

Fifty States, Fifty Weeks

walkie-talkie so we could communicate at all times. The same held true for Melinda when she went for a run.

As an urban guy, I found spending time in the wilderness unsettling in some ways unsettling. In a city, people are always around, which can be a comfort because you know someone is nearby in case of emergency. There is at least a feeling of safety in numbers. At Denali, I found myself becoming hypervigilant—feeling the full weight of responsibility for the safety of my wife and sons. Moreover, I started to think, *I can't believe I left my job and we're here in the middle of nowhere. How could I have done this to my family?*

Yes, doubts abounded during our trip to Denali. We had come to this almost surreal place of mountains and glaciers, a place so different from the hustle and bustle of our California lifestyle that the full weight of my decision hit me. Wow, I had really done this and had ended up here, in what seemed to be a million miles away from civilization. Well, as long as we were here, we might as well embrace the experience, the challenges, and the discoveries.

Traveling through Denali, I again pondered the pioneers: people who had put fear aside and embarked on a journey into the unknown in a primitive mode of transportation, with no one waiting for them at the end of the trail, and people who took risks and created new paths. Thinking about these American heroes never failed to give me strength and courage.

George Arredondo

On August 11, we packed up and headed back to Anchorage. As we approached the city, I asked Melinda and the boys if they'd prefer to spend the evening relaxing at the hotel or to make a seventy-five-mile detour to Whittier, Alaska, a sister city to our final destination, Whittier, California, where my three fellow travelers were born. All agreed to take the exit and check out our town's namesake in Alaska, the Last Frontier. I was happy and proud that we all felt a growing spirit of adventure.

To reach Whittier, Alaska, like our hometown named for the poet John Greenleaf Whittier, we had to travel through the Anton Anderson Memorial Tunnel, a one-and-a-half-mile tunnel through Maynard Mountain, the second-longest highway tunnel in North America. Good thing none of us suffer from claustrophobia.

Located southeast of Anchorage on Prince William Sound, Whittier is a port city, with a population of around two hundred people. During our visit, we stopped for ice cream, snapped a photo of the town marker, and then headed back to Anchorage. It was a long way to go for ice cream and a photograph, but the visit to our sister city turned out to be one of the major talking points of fifty states in fifty weeks. We told the story over and over, and people always found it fascinating.

We spent the next day, August 12, in Anchorage, visiting the University of Alaska and exploring the city's downtown area. The most exciting part of our stay in Anchorage was having dinner with the boys' cousin Veronica, who has lived in Alaska for a few years. It was great to see her after a long, long time.

On August 13, we flew back to Seattle and settled into a hotel for a few days to enjoy a bit of pampering after our Alaskan wilderness adventure. Now that we were in a major metropolis, we had to partake of our favorite form of recreation: attending a Major League Baseball game. We headed to Safeco Field, where we saw the Tampa Bay Rays beat the Seattle Mariners four to one. As we sat in the stadium for the night game, it was comforting to watch the sun set at a "normal" time. In Alaska, it seemed as if the sun never really set.

Fifty States, Fifty Weeks

The following day, we enjoyed just hanging out together without anything big on the agenda. However, the next morning, I felt obliged to show the boys some local culture and offered to take them to several museums while their mother had some time to herself. As an afterthought, I said, "Or we can go to the baseball game." I didn't think they'd pick the game, since we'd already visited the ballpark and could cross it off our list of Major League stadiums.

Gavin picked up the newspaper—I'd imparted my love for the sports pages to both of my sons—and said, "The King is pitching today." He was referring to Felix Hernandez, a twenty-six-year-old superstar pitcher from Venezuela who'd won the Cy Young Award in 2010 as the best pitcher in the American League. Both boys wanted to attend the game, and I was pleased that they'd made this choice because that was what I really wanted to do.

When we stepped up to the booth to purchase the tickets, the vendor offered us a variety of prime seats on the lower decks, but Gavin, as usual, requested seats behind home plate in the last row of the top deck. Garon and I would have preferred sitting on a lower level, but we went along with Gavin. He just loved the top perch, where he could see everything and take in not just the game but also the crowd, the stadium, and the surroundings.

Even though we were at a sporting event, I still felt as if I were in my working mode because I am a serious, and I mean capital-*S* Serious, baseball fan. So are the boys.

For my eleventh birthday, my workaholic father took me to a Dodgers game. I remember two things about the event: It was the only time my father ever took me to a baseball game, and we left early—a matter of bitter disappointment for me. I promised my sons that during their childhood, I'd take them to probably hundreds of games and we would never leave early.

That day, Felix Hernandez made history by pitching a perfect game, only the twenty-third in Major League Baseball history. A perfect game is defined as a game that lasts at least nine innings where no opposing player reaches base. A few innings before the end of the game, the crowd started to rumble with excitement, which grew as Hernandez hurled each pitch. The fans became like a force, urging Hernandez toward this once-in-a-career accomplishment. After it was all over, Garon and I were glad we'd allowed Gavin to choose the seats because we were able to snap a perfect picture at the perfect game.

That night, while we were digging into a scrumptious dinner at the Space Needle, our server noticed that the boys were both wearing Hernandez jerseys that featured the pitcher's name and number thirty-four. The server said, "The King pitched a perfect game today."

Without hesitation, Gavin piped up, "We were there. We were part of history."

Our server was so impressed that he replied, "Dessert's on me!"

The next day, August 16, the boys started their homeschooling while we drove to Moses Lake (about three hours southeast of Seattle), which is the name of the city and its namesake body of water. By the time we reached our destination, Garon and Gavin had completed their schoolwork, and they were ready for a swim.

The following morning, we headed for state number five: Idaho, the Gem State. On the way, we made a final stop in Washington, enjoying a tasty lunch at a Mexican restaurant in Spokane. The drive from

Washington to Idaho was spectacular: purple mountains, green forests, blue skies, silver lakes, and golden sunshine. The beautiful scenery made me wish I could paint; only a gifted artist could capture the spell that the surroundings exerted on us.

On August 17, we rolled into Coeur d'Alene, a city in the Idaho panhandle, located on the shore of Lake Coeur d'Alene. This is a major vacation spot, with all types of water sports, including water biking and white-water rafting on the Coeur d'Alene River, in a magnificent setting. I had to remind myself not to fall into the vacation mind-set. For one thing, I had to decide what to do about the RV. I was now convinced that we had to make a change but wasn't sure how to go about it.

We fell in love with Coeur d'Alene and had a total blast the three days we spent there, exploring the gorgeous surroundings, splashing in the waterways, and just hanging out together. A culinary highlight was eating—several times—at Hudson's Hamburgers, probably the best burgers in the world. One night, Garon, who was working on his Boy Scout camping merit badge, cooked dinner for us, and we finished off the evening by watching *RV*, starring Robin Williams, a 2006 movie that was more meaningful and seemed funnier now than the first time we'd seen it a few years back.

George Arredondo

August 20 marked us entering our sixth state: Montana, Big Sky Country. We arrived in Trout Creek, the huckleberry capital of Montana, located near the northwest corner of the state. While there, we sampled huckleberries (round berries similar in taste and appearance to blueberries) in many forms, including pancakes, smoothies, and ice cream.

After driving south for about 120 miles, that night we settled into a Jellystone Park RV camp, a national chain named for the fictional place where the cartoon character Yogi Bear lives, in Missoula, Montana. Garon and Gavin loved this kidcentric site, which featured swimming, a game arcade, miniature golf water slides, and wagon rides.

The next day, we headed north, about fifty miles from the Canadian border, for Kalispell, where Garon visited Boy Scout Troop 1933. As troop ambassador in his home troop, he was scheduled to visit troops throughout the country. The boys in Troop 1933 gave Garon a warm welcome.

As we drove the highways and byways, Garon and Gavin did most of their schoolwork. Bit by bit they were getting into the learning mode, though it wasn't always easy to watch DVDs and complete written assignments while the RV was bouncing around.

I figured we'd better do something about our vehicle before we set off for Yellowstone National Park, with its steep passages. Throughout the trip, our RV had lagged when ascending mountains and even hills. I needed to talk to Melinda about making a switch. As soon as I brought up the subject, Melinda let out a big sigh of relief. She'd been thinking the same thing: We needed an RV like the one we'd driven in Alaska. "Changing RVs is going to cost us," I said. "It won't be cheap." She told me it was my decision.

My job was to get my family back to Whittier safe and sound, so I decided to trade down our vehicle and get us into a twenty-four-foot C-class RV that was lower to the ground and easier to maneuver. The decision cost us over $10,000, but it was worth every penny in comfort, convenience, and peace of mind.

The experience made me realize that sometimes you have to start down the road before you understand what you need, and you can't expect to know everything before you take off. This was a valuable lesson for all of us: a good leader recognizes when to make an adjustment.

I felt as if a huge weight had been lifted off my shoulders as we piled into our new RV and zoomed toward one of America's crown jewels: Yellowstone National Park.

CHAPTER 5

Slow Down

On September 1, we marked the one-month anniversary of fifty states in fifty weeks with a three-hour drive from Sioux Falls, South Dakota, to Wahpeton, North Dakota, located in the state's southeast corner. We decided to celebrate the official end of summer—Labor Day weekend—by having each of us choose an activity. Melinda was first to offer her request. She wanted to stay in a hotel so she could focus on paperwork related to our real-estate business and the boys' homeschooling, plus catch up on laundry and sleep. The boys and I were glad for lodgings that were more spacious—we enjoyed spreading out too!

When we arrived in Wahpeton, population eight thousand, we took a spin through this all-American community, with its pristine downtown area, manicured parks, and array of historic sites and museums. Later, as we prepared to exit the RV and check into the hotel, Melinda placed the sticker for the Peace Garden State, the ninth state we'd visited, on our RV map.

As their Labor Day weekend picks, Garon and Gavin chose to play electronic games and then visit the Chahinkapa Zoo, an impressive eighteen-acre setting that houses over two hundred animals, including endangered species. We were amazed that a town the size of Wahpeton featured such an extensive, modern zoo. As we wove our way through the animal exhibits, I thought of Noah's preparation for his journey on the ark. Traveling across America in an RV, I felt a special kinship with the patriarch and his menagerie.

The next day, we all decided to chill in our own ways. Melinda and Gavin opted to hang out in the hotel while Garon and I took off for the nearby Bois De Sioux Golf Course. I was looking forward to visiting the course because it offered the chance to play in two states, since the front nine holes are located in North Dakota and the back nine in Minnesota.

However, a more important aspect of the excursion involved Garon; it had been a while since I'd spent any quality one-on-one time with him. I asked him if he wanted to tee off with me, but he preferred to watch me hack away. Then I got a brainstorm. One of my goals for the trip was to teach Garon to drive, and why not start with a golf cart? He was my official caddy for the day—an activity that he really liked. The thing about golf is you spend more time traveling between holes than you do actually playing the game, which was the perfect setup for some father/son discussions with Garon. As I showed him how to drive the golf cart, which he picked up right away, and we rode from hole to hole, we got a chance to engage in some in-depth conversations about how he felt about the trip and the homeschooling. I also took time to explain that it was important for him to serve as an example to his brother by sharing his love of reading with Gavin and watching over him when Melinda and I took walks together.

We finished the eighteenth hole in Minnesota and then made our way back to the clubhouse in North Dakota. I'd completed the game in record time—not because I'd made numerous holes in one or bogeys or because Garon sped the golf cart around the green. We'd zipped through the eighteen holes because the course was virtually deserted.

Driving back to the hotel, I realized that the whole town seemed somewhat abandoned, and I wondered if the residents were spending the last official weekend of summer either at home or at a recreational area. As we drove around town, we passed one of Wahpeton's must-sees: a forty-foot-long, twelve-foot-tall roadside attraction named "Wahpper," dubbed the world's largest catfish.

While traveling across the country, we'd seen—and would continue to see—many features designated as the "world's largest," "best," or "only" or places named the "capital of the world" for some local feat. Part of the fun of traveling was discovering things in a local community we never would have imagined existed, let alone qualified as a marvel of the world.

After a leisurely afternoon of golf, I felt relaxed and ready to get back on the road, and I couldn't wait for the next day so we could take off. I hated idle time; it gave me too much time to think. When I started thinking, my mind turned to the job I'd left in June. After ten weeks away from the daily grind, I still had not mentally detached from my employer. I replayed scenes over and over in my mind, trying to understand why and how the job had degenerated into one where I had no choice but to walk away.

It didn't help that I kept in contact with fellow employees via texts and e-mails, and these former coworkers were only too willing to fill me in on the latest details. They were also following our blog—one of Melinda's daily responsibilities was writing the posts and uploading photos to the site—and often asked questions about the trip, most notably, "When are you going to be finished?"

I started to ask myself the same question because after a month on the road, I began to feel anxious about my career and financial prospects, fretting that we were going to run out of money and that I'd better line up a job before the trip was over. Additionally, now that we were out of our comfort zone—the Western states—and were entering the unfamiliar Midwest, I was concerned about staying ahead of bad weather.

In California and much of the Western United States, the weather is fairly constant year-round, with few extremes in the form of snowstorms, thunderstorms, tornadoes, hurricanes, hailstorms, flash floods, or any of the other conditions that beset the Midwest, East, and South. Now we were about to enter the erratic weather zone, and thoughts of driving in treacherous conditions and keeping my family safe filled me with concern.

On Labor Day, we headed for Minnesota, and I drove without stopping for about three hours to the Minneapolis/Saint Paul area, even though I'd spotted what looked like a few points of interest along the way—for one, the Stearns History Museum in Saint Cloud, Minnesota. I made a decision not to take the exit or make a detour because I was in a hurry to reach our destination.

Fifty States, Fifty Weeks

We decided to stay in a hotel for a few days, and as I placed the sticker for the Land of Ten Thousand Lakes on our RV map, it hit me that we had crossed ten states off our list in just one month. We were already in double digits, and, at this rate, we'd be finished by the end of December, completing the trip in twenty weeks rather than the planned fifty weeks.

Later, when the boys were completing some of their homeschooling work, Melinda took me aside and told me I needed to slow down and stop rushing from point *A* to point *B*.

"How many times will we take a trip like this?" she asked me.

"Once," I replied.

"Then we need to take our time," she said.

I knew she was right and admitted that I was still in job mode and operating in fifth gear. One of my strengths in business was my ability to get things done fast. I'd been speeding along, making plans, crossing things off the list, and accomplishing goals since starting work thirty-five years before. I now understood that I'd approached the trip as a project and was so busy keeping track of miles driven, states visited, and dollars spent that I was missing the point of the trip. Our goal wasn't to rush from place to place just to say that we'd been there but to experience each state, to learn new things about our country, and to gain insights into ourselves.

Labor Day was a time for me to let go of my previous labors and focus on the here and now, to slow down and welcome the unknown and new adventures—even if they involved inclement weather.

To get some practice as a mellow, laid-back traveler, I suggested that we spend about five days exploring the Minneapolis/Saint Paul area. Melinda was pleased that I was slowing down our pace, and the boys were excited about spending part of their allowance at the world's largest shopping center—without me hurrying them through the stores.

Even though our hotel in Bloomington was across the street from the Mall of America, we didn't visit the shopping mecca for a few days—the promised trip was a great incentive for the boys to apply themselves in their schoolwork.

George Arredondo

On September 4, Garon attended a Boy Scout meeting with Troop 437, where he felt welcome and traded a council patch.

As a preview for our extended visit to the Mall of America, we did a preliminary walk-through on the evening of September 5. We took in the lay of the land and the gigantic dimensions of the place, which is big enough to fit seven Yankee Stadiums, and were glad that our athletic shoes were already broken in so we could get started right away the following afternoon.

After school the next day, we took off for our shopping excursion at Minnesota's most popular tourist attraction, which boasts forty million visitors each year. Completed in 1992, the Mall of America now features over five hundred stores and restaurants, plus an amusement park, an aquarium, and a multiplex theater.

We bought day passes for the seven-acre Nickelodeon Universe, an indoor amusement park with four roller coasters and an assortment of other rides. As baseball fanatics, we started by riding the SpongeBob Square Pants Rock Bottom Plunge roller coaster, where the floor outside the ride features the home plate for the Minnesota Twins' old playing field, Metropolitan Stadium, which once stood on the site.

Now that I'd vowed to slow down and stop rushing, I found myself on a variety of whirling, spinning, blasting, speeding rides that made my head spin and my stomach churn. These amusements seemed to reflect, in a fun-house way, the kind of life I'd been living for so many years: fast, frenetic, and filled with unexpected twists and turns. Despite the jostling I received on these rides, which Garon insisted that Melinda and I join in on, I felt myself slowing down. I wasn't in a hurry to get anywhere or in a rush to do anything. In fact, I kept showing my day-pass wristband and going back for more shaking, rattling, and rolling on the rides, feeling as if I were getting rid of some of my residual job angst through centrifugal force.

Other highlights of the day included a trip to the Lego Store, where Gavin bought a new set of the colorful blocks, and a visit to the SEA LIFE Minnesota Aquarium, home to more than ten thousand sea creatures, including sharks, stingrays, and sea turtles, where we saw the world's largest jellyfish collection.

We stayed so long at the Mall of America that we ate two meals there. It was dark by the time we got back to our hotel, and we were pretty sure we'd walked at least five miles touring the megamall.

The next morning, we visited Target Field, located in downtown Minneapolis, home of the Minnesota Twins since 2010, and saw the Cleveland Indians sweat out a victory, beating the home team seven to six in an exciting game. This was the second Major League Baseball park that we'd visited during the trip—and this one had special meaning for Gavin, since it was named for his favorite retailer, which was headquartered in the area. On the way back to our hotel in Bloomington, we drove by the Target corporate offices in Minneapolis so Gavin could pay his respects.

We'd started our trip in the Target parking lot in Roseville, California, and we'd already made it as far as the "Expect More. Pay Less" home base. In a little over a month, we'd traveled thousands of miles; the straight distance from Sacramento to Minneapolis is almost two thousand miles, and we had wound around and taken a detour to Alaska, so I figured we'd already piled on at least five thousand miles. As I'd realized a few days earlier, we needed to slow down.

I made a promise to myself—and to my family—to adapt the Target slogan to our trip: "Less Speed. More Fun."

CHAPTER 6

Take the Exit

AFTER A THREE-AND-A-HALF-HOUR drive from Minneapolis, we arrived in Wisconsin Dells, a five-mile gorge on the Wisconsin River renowned for its sandstone rock formations and located in south-central Wisconsin, our eleventh state (nicknamed the Badger State).

We had traveled nonstop from Minneapolis. I was already breaking my vow to slow down and take the exit, but we were booked to stay at the Mount Olympus Resort, where a coveted treehouse awaited us. With only a few of these arbor abodes in the entire RV park, they are in high demand, and if we didn't show up at the appointed time, we risked forfeiting the accommodations as well as our deposit. If all this sounds like an excuse for not taking the exit, it's just a way of showing that my spirit was willing but duty called.

Our first experience with extreme Midwestern weather was a torrential downpour on the day we arrived. There was also a chill in the air, giving us a hint of the fall season, something that, as Californians, we'd never experienced in our "autumnless" home state. We got snug in our tree house—a rustic cabin set on a fabricated tree trunk—and the boys did two days' worth of homeschooling so we'd be free the next day to explore Mount Olympus Water and Theme Park.

Our arrival occurred the weekend after Labor Day, when the vacation season was over and the local kids were back in school, and just a few stragglers were left, including the Arredondo family, enjoying a last hurrah of summer.

Mount Olympus is designated as the world's largest water-and-theme-park resort—another "world's largest" something. Like its name, the park features attractions named for people and places in Greek mythology: Zeus's Playground, Neptune's Water Kingdom, the Parthenon, Medusa's Indoor Water Park, and the Trojan Horse Go-Kart Track.

On Sunday, September 9, the sun was shining, the temperature was a pleasant seventy-five, and the water was cold—but that didn't deter us from exploring the Wisconsin River and the aquatic rides. Garon even coaxed me onto the scream-inducing Cyclops roller coaster. With no lines for the rides and few people around us, we felt as if Mount Olympus were our private playground. We had such a great time that we spent two days at the park.

On Monday afternoon, we took a beautiful two-hour drive to Milwaukee through the state's verdant countryside. What a difference rain makes! We didn't see green like this in California. The landscape in Wisconsin was so lush that it looked like a painting.

While we drove, the boys did their schoolwork. As we approached Milwaukee's downtown area, Gavin asked his mother if he could stop working for a while and look at the skyline because he really enjoys viewing the downtown areas of large cities. Melinda was happy to comply and glad to learn this new fact about her youngest son.

After checking into a hotel, we headed to Miller Park for a game between the Milwaukee Brewers and the Atlanta Braves. The Brewers beat the Braves four to one, making the hometown crowd proud, especially since the Braves had been a Milwaukee team from 1953–1965. Miller Park, the third baseball stadium we'd visited during the trip, was a magnificent structure that had been completed in 2001 and had a retractable roof that could open and close in ten minutes. When you live in a high-precipitation state, I guess that's a sure way to avoid rain delays.

I was eager to take off for Chicago, one of my favorite big cities, but Melinda again advised that we slow down. We were in Milwaukee, so why not explore it? She also mentioned that we'd attended Major League Baseball games during the past week and would attend a few more in Chicago, and she felt it was time for a cultural activity. I had to agree with her, so we took off for downtown Milwaukee, enjoying a walk along the city's magnificent lakefront before we visited the Milwaukee Art Museum.

At this huge, modern museum near the shore of Lake Michigan, we saw some of the world's most renowned works of art, including paintings by Claude Monet, Winslow Homer, and Andy Warhol. However, what captivated my attention and imagination and gave me a feeling of déjà vu were two exhibits, one called *Painters of the American West* and the other made up of Ansel Adams photographs, in which the images reflected places we had just visited.

Paying a visit to the Milwaukee Art Museum, which I had intended to bypass in favor of a drive to Chicago, and seeing the places we'd visited as depicted by master artists made me realize God's hand in planning our trip. I could see and feel the Almighty's wise guidance and felt humble and grateful that God had blessed us. More than ever, I felt the truth of our motto: "Exploring America with faith and family."

The next day, September 12, we drove to Illinois, the Prairie State, and stayed at an RV park about thirty miles from downtown Chicago. We spent the rest of the day there, with the boys working on their schoolwork and getting a bit ahead so we had enough free time to explore Chicago during the coming days. I was also starting to understand that it was easier for Garon and Gavin to do their work while we were in a stationary position, since their DVD players bounced around and it was difficult to complete written assignments in an RV zooming down the road at fifty-five miles an hour.

The following morning, we rented a car and booked a hotel room near downtown Chicago. Garon and Gavin were excited about visiting another city with two Major League Baseball teams. We were proud that Los Angeles had two MLB teams and were looking forward to visiting two-team New York. As we drove toward Chicago's spectacular skyline, Gavin gave the buildings his full attention, without schoolwork to distract him.

We started our tour of the Windy City with a high-speed elevator ride to the top of Willis Tower (formerly known as Sears Tower), the tallest building in the Western Hemisphere at the time. From the observation desk, you could see four states: Illinois, Indiana, Wisconsin, and Michigan. The boys were happy to add "tallest building" to their list of superlative places they'd visited.

Garon and Gavin are both interested in architecture, and Chicago gave them opportunities to view the work of renowned architects, including Louis Sullivan, Frank Lloyd Wright, and Ludwig Mies van der Rohe.

Many years before, Melinda and I had spent a weekend in Chicago, so we were looking forward to repeating one of our favorite experiences: digging into a deep-dish Chicago-style pizza. The forty-minute wait at Giordano's was worth it—wow! Pizza lovers, you haven't lived until you've enjoyed one of these monsters.

That night, we made our way to US Cellular Field (formerly called Comiskey Park) to see the Chicago White Sox play the Detroit Tigers. While we prefer National League games—go Dodgers!—we were pleased to add another stadium to our list of Major League Baseball parks visited.

We were still getting used to the unpredictable weather in the Midwest, with sudden shifts in temperature and cloudbursts accompanied by lightning and thunder. After ninety minutes, the game was called because of rain, and while we were disappointed, at least we'd seen the stadium.

George Arredondo

It was another story at Wrigley Field, home of the Chicago Cubs, where we attended games on subsequent days. The country's second-oldest MLB park (Fenway Park in Boston takes top spot), Wrigley Field opened in 1914, and its ivy-covered walls have hosted the game's greatest players. Garon remarked on the park's relatively small size compared to today's stadiums and marveled that it was situated in the middle of a busy residential area. He observed that a century ago, baseball parks were touchstones in their communities—the way schools, churches, and libraries were vital anchors—and this was one of the reasons that the sport took hold and thrived.

Garon's comments about baseball sparked me to check out the Dodgers' schedule and see if any games were scheduled in Chicago. I learned that our home team—and we were really starting to miss watching their games—was playing in Cincinnati the following week.

Fifty States, Fifty Weeks

The next logical state after Illinois was Indiana, but I figured if we looped south through Illinois to Saint Louis, we could hit Missouri and then loop back through Kentucky and up to Cincinnati. This unscheduled jaunt—a thousand miles off the planned route—was a long, winding path to the Dodgers game in Cincinnati. However, it felt like the right thing to do. I asked Melinda and the boys what they thought, and my fellow travelers were all for the side trip, the first time we had deviated from the logical route.

I thought we'd drive about two hundred miles to the state capital, Springfield, spend a few hours there, and then travel another hundred miles to Saint Louis and stay a few days there. However, about ninety miles from Chicago, I saw a sign that said, "Eureka College, Alma Mater of Ronald Reagan," and decided to take the exit.

It turned out that Eureka College was nowhere near the exit but another fifty miles down a two-lane road. As I did during most of my driving, I listened to an audiobook—the boys were far enough away, in the back of the RV, that my book didn't interfere with their lessons, which they listened to with headphones.

At around two in the afternoon, we reached Ronald Reagan's alma mater—a quaint, tree-lined, well-kept campus with redbrick buildings built in a style that harkened back to 1855, when the college was founded. As we walked the campus, I mentioned to Melinda that before long we'd need to take another road trip to help Garon decide where to go to college. She told me to slow down—we needed to finish this trip first.

I thought back to my own experiences with higher education. Considering all the turmoil I'd experienced living with my father during my high-school years, I was lucky I graduated and was even one of the valedictory speakers. However, I had neither the money nor the overall grades to qualify for a scholarship, so I had to go to work full time—as a manager at Kmart—and attend junior college in the evenings. After graduating from junior college, I enrolled in the adult program at the University of Southern California and studied business administration at night while continuing to work a full-time job. I was the second in my family, after my brother David, to graduate from college. However, I sometimes feel nostalgia for something I never experienced: a carefree, financed four-year journey through a university, where I could attend classes during the day and study at night. I was proud that Melinda and I could provide this experience for our two sons.

While visiting the Ronald Reagan Museum on the Eureka College campus, I learned some surprising facts about our fortieth president. For one thing, he grew up poor and worked summers as a lifeguard, saving every cent to pay for his college education. The museum focused on Reagan's career at Eureka College, from 1928–1932. Somehow, he managed to get an education during the height of the Great Depression, as a student, athlete, and campus leader.

I was so inspired by Reagan's rags-to-riches story that I wanted to know more. As soon as we returned to the RV, I ordered a Kindle version of his autobiography, entitled *Where's the Rest of Me?*

We also learned at Eureka College that the state of Illinois boasts four US presidents—Lincoln, Grant, Reagan, and Obama—and the guide at the Reagan Museum suggested that we explore some of the Lincoln sites in Springfield.

When we got back on the road, I saw signs for the Lincoln Heritage Museum in Lincoln, Illinois, and figured that two museums dedicated to presidents in one day would be even better than two Major League Baseball games in one day—hear that, Melinda?

Fifty States, Fifty Weeks

About an hour later, we arrived in the city of Lincoln, where Abraham Lincoln practiced law from 1847–1859. The city also boasts the interesting distinction of being the only US city that was named for Lincoln before he was elected the nation's sixteenth president in 1860. The Lincoln Heritage Museum houses a collection of artifacts that tell the story of Lincoln's life and features portraits, campaign memorabilia, and even furniture from his home. It was easy to feel close to this heroic and popular president when exploring objects from his everyday life.

For me, Lincoln is a particular inspiration because he came from a humble background and was a self-made businessman and, later, a self-educated lawyer. As we viewed the museum displays, I explained to the boys how Lincoln and Reagan had excelled through hard work and effort—that was one of the greatest things about our country: Everyone had at least a chance to reach the top of any field through personal diligence and a few heroes along the way. I took this chance to mention how my brother David had served as my inspiration and guide, and I gave their uncle major credit for any success I'd achieved in my educational and business careers.

Visiting the museums dedicated to Reagan and Lincoln really brought home why we were taking this trip: to get to know our country, our history, and our heroes in more depth and to be inspired. When we left the Lincoln Heritage Museum, I felt proud to live in a land where anybody could rise to the top and make a difference in the world.

An hour later, we reached Springfield, the state capital and home to many renowned Lincoln sites, including the Lincoln Presidential Library and Museum—an ultramodern facility opened in 2005—and Honest Abe's personal residence at Eighth and Jackson, where he and his family lived for seventeen years. Both Garon and Gavin—and Mom and Dad—agreed that Lincoln was their favorite president.

When we got back on the road, the boys resumed their schoolwork. Melinda had recently agreed to allow them to do their written work when we arrived at a destination because it was just too difficult to write in a moving RV. According to their mom (and teacher), they were doing a great job and were right on schedule. Melinda prepared classwork, quizzes, and tests the night before and graded all the work each day. On her blog post for September 12, Melinda wrote, "In addition to the classwork, the boys have been getting a great hands-on education, visiting many places throughout the United States. As we approach different states, we try to learn a little about that particular state."

We stopped for the night at an RV park and then took off the next morning for Saint Louis. On September 18, we crossed the Mississippi River and entered Missouri, the Show Me State.

We had an action-packed day in Saint Louis, starting out with a ride on a Mississippi riverboat—technically a paddle steamer, a vessel equipped with a steam engine that drove paddle wheels that propelled the vehicle forward—a mode of transportation that harkens back to the eighteen hundreds. It was fun riding the mighty Mississippi—our nation's longest river, which bisects the country vertically—and imaging what life was like in the early nineteenth century, when Saint Louis was the last point of civilization before people headed to the western frontier.

My architecture-buff sons couldn't wait to get to the Gateway Arch to explore this magnificent structure, the tallest manufactured monument in the United States and, at 630 feet, the world's tallest arch. Of course, we had to take the ride up in small enclosures that seemed to inch their way to the top, where you could look down through tiny windows. As soon as we glanced out the windows, Melinda told us she was ready to leave. While the view of the river and surrounding area was breathtaking, the closed atmosphere in the arch was a bit unsettling, so we took the next seats down.

The Gateway Arch is a component of the Jefferson National Expansion Memorial, which also includes the Museum of Westward Expansion. The site commemorates the Louisiana Purchase, which facilitated the western movement of explorers and pioneers, and was named for US President Thomas Jefferson, who was instrumental in purchasing a nearly one-million-square-mile tract of land from France in 1803 in what is now the Western United States.

As I stood on the banks of the Mississippi and looked west, it occurred to me that there will always be new frontiers if you're willing to slow down, stop, and take the exit.

Later in the afternoon, Garon attended a Boy Scout meeting with local Troup 473, where he told the story of our trip—up to and including our thirteenth state. The people in the audience gave him their full attention and had plenty of questions and comments, including the now-familiar, "You're so lucky." I think Garon was starting to believe it!

For Gavin, the highlight of the day occurred a few hours later, when we attended a game at Busch Stadium—at one time, the home field of Albert Pujols, one of Gavin's favorite players. We cheered with the crowd as the Cardinals beat the Houston Astros five to zero, and we added another MLB park to our list.

The next morning, we drove east, across Illinois, and entered Indiana, our fourteenth state, nicknamed the Hoosier State. We got off the highways and took the byways, touring the luxuriant farmland of vivid shades of green—you'll never know the color green until you see plants growing in an area that gets lots of rain. (I guess that's why they call Ireland the Emerald Isle.) We were truly in our nation's heartland, and I understood why the Midwest is nicknamed the nation's breadbasket, since most of our staples (corn, wheat, soybeans, and oats) are grown there.

As we headed down the road, we saw a sign that we just couldn't resist and had no choice but to take the exit—I mean, you'd have to be a Scrooge or Grinch to resist a town called Santa Claus. Even though the weather was warm, the Christmas spirit was alive and well in Santa Claus, Indiana, where all the streets had winter-inspired names and the shops featured yuletide cheer in the form of ornaments and Christmas cards.

Thinking ahead, we purchased some ornaments for our Christmas in the RV. Yes, we would still be on the road at Christmastime and beyond, putting to rest my recent fear that we would finish the trip in December. We would take exits and detours and extend our adventure well into the new year.

CHAPTER 7

I Don't Know; Let's Find Out

My favorite—and the most challenging—aspect of the trip was driving the RV. While road conditions, weather changes, and heavy traffic tested my alertness and driving ability, navigating the roads of America enhanced my confidence and appreciation for people who drive vehicles for a living.

However, beyond the sense of accomplishment and purpose I derived from commanding the RV, I enjoyed even more another aspect of driving: the moving vehicle's meditative rhythm that put me in a frame of mind to ponder the past, appreciate the present, and look forward to the future.

About ninety days had passed since I'd left my job in Northern California, and I was finally starting to decompress and look at the situation with more perspective and self-reflection. I realized that for fifteen years, I'd been afraid to utter the words, "I don't know." I was paid—and well compensated—to know everything that affected operations in our business. However, my need to "know it all" spilled over into most areas of my life, even with my kids. If they asked a question and I didn't know the answer, I just spouted off something from the top of my head. I couldn't say the words "I don't know" to my boss, my sons, or my wife.

I don't believe I was consciously acting in a dishonest or devious manner. In a way, I'd been on autopilot—just trying to get through the day without any major collisions. One way to avoid conflict or confrontation was to act as if all was well, as if I had all the answers and would handle everything that came along.

During the past few years, Melinda had tried to call me on my know-it-all bravado, especially since she'd noticed Garon and Gavin emulating me by making something up or taking shortcuts with homework rather than finding the answer. However, for the most part, I was in denial and tried to turn things around to make it seem as if Melinda were making a big deal out of nothing.

While watching the white line on the highway, I had time to reflect on the past few years and finally understood what Melinda had been talking about. On a trip like ours—with a myriad of daily unknowns—it was impossible to fake knowing it all.

September 21 was Garon's thirteenth birthday—and we'd just entered our fifteenth state, Kentucky, the Blue Grass State. As we crossed the state border, I was hoping my conavigator wouldn't ask how the state had gotten its nickname; I didn't know but was not yet ready to admit I did not know.

We'd planned some special activities to celebrate Garon's milestone birthday. He was now a teenager (time really does fly!) but was still a baseball fanatic. Our first stop was the Louisville Slugger Museum & Factory, where the company manufactures the official bat of Major League Baseball. In business for over a century and still owned by the original family, the site displays bats that belonged to iconic players in baseball history. On display is the custom Louisville Slugger Babe Ruth used to hit sixty home runs during his record-setting 1927 season—and the bat features a notch Ruth made for each homer. What an honor to view this priceless artifact!

After a ninety-minute drive, we settled into an RV park in Covington, Kentucky, a short walk from the Great American Stadium, home of the Cincinnati Reds. I was thrilled that we could treat Garon to a Dodgers game on his special day and so glad I'd followed my instincts and deviated from the expected route so we could make his thirteenth birthday one he'd never forget. Furthermore, unlike my eleventh birthday at Dodger Stadium, we would not leave early.

As we walked to the stadium across the Roebling Suspension Bridge, a thoroughfare dating from 1866 that spans the Ohio River, Garon remarked on the impressive structure, saying he was intrigued by the bridge's design and construction and it inspired him to think about becoming an architect. This was the first time that Garon had discussed the career path he wanted to explore, and I was gratified that the trip had provided a source of inspiration.

After the game—our team was victorious in a ten-inning three-to-one matchup—the bridge's blue suspension wires, lit up at night, made us think of our team's color. We felt triumphant as we crossed back to Kentucky.

During the weekend of September 22 and 23, we saw two more games between the Dodgers and the Reds, with each team claiming a victory and the Dodgers getting the best two out of three.

Cincinnati celebrated the beginning of autumn with an Oktoberfest extravaganza—the largest Oktoberfest in the United States. The city transforms itself into "Zinzinnati," and over a half million people take part in the festivities. We had fun checking out the food and the people in lederhosen dancing the beer-barrel polka and the Chicken Dance. I'm not comfortable in situations where beer flows in torrents, so we didn't stick around longer than to say, "Been there, done that."

I'll admit that we've left many family gatherings early or have chosen not to attend because neither Melinda nor I drink alcoholic beverages, but I explained to my sons, "You make choices, and you have to accept the consequences."

Growing up, I felt that my father considered his eight children less important than his job or his drinking. How could I think otherwise since we garnered little of his attention, and his work and alcohol consumed all of his time? While I became close to my father during his later years, you can never turn back the clock and regain the time you've missed. I had grown up without a father, and even though I didn't drink, I had gotten precariously close to abandoning my sons in favor of my career—until I had come to my senses when I'd left my job about three months before.

On Monday, September 24, we got back on the road and headed north. After driving for about two hours, I saw a sign for the Armstrong Air and Space Museum in Wapakoneta, Ohio. I'd read that Neil Armstrong

George Arredondo

(the first man to walk on the moon in 1969) had passed away about a month earlier, and I decided to take the exit and visit the hometown of this American hero.

I knew almost nothing about Neil Armstrong, other than his celebrated lunar stroll, and when I got off the interstate, my copilot, Garon, filled in some details, sharing that Armstrong had been active in the Boy Scouts, earning the rank of Eagle Scout and carrying the World Scout emblem with him to the moon and back. Since we had now shared everything we knew about Armstrong, I said, "Let's find out more."

At the Armstrong Air and Space Museum, we learned not only about the renowned astronaut but also about space exploration. Displays included several suits Armstrong had worn in space, a rock gathered on the moon, and space simulators. We learned that at the time of his 1969 walk on the moon, Neil Armstrong was designated as a civilian pilot since he'd left military service in 1960. I mentioned to Gavin and Garon that Armstrong represented each American, and as he took those steps into the unknown, he was showing all of us that we needed to always forge ahead into new frontiers. He'd made the American people and the Boy Scouts of America very proud.

After driving for about an hour to Van Buren, Ohio—named for Martin Van Buren, the eighth president of the United States—we settled in for the evening, the boys completing their school assignments while I grilled some chicken for dinner. Melinda, as usual, was busy, uploading entries and photos to our blog, doing paperwork related to our real-estate holdings, and correcting school papers, plus cleaning the RV and doing laundry. Other than driving, acting as tour guide, and barbecuing, my other major contribution was hooking up the RV's sewage lines when we parked for the day. This not-too-pleasant activity gave me a greater appreciation for people who work in all types of service jobs, people I'd taken for granted not that long ago.

The next day, we entered our seventeenth state—Michigan, the Wolverine State. I don't think I'm alone in saying, "I don't know; let's find out," when it comes to wolverines. For the record, according to *Webster's* dictionary, a wolverine is "a heavily built, short-legged carnivorous mammal with a shaggy, dark coat and a bushy tail, native to the tundra and forests of arctic and subarctic regions." These are some scary-looking beasts that remind me of a cross between a raccoon and a bear.

In the Northern states, the camping season had passed, and few RV parks were open for business. When we reached Detroit, we headed downtown and booked a room at GM Towers (the Detroit Marriott), located just a few miles from Comerica Park, home of the Detroit Tigers. We enjoyed cheering with the crowd as the Tigers beat the Royals, the win putting the team in a tie for first place in the American League Central Division. (The Tigers would go on to win the American League pennant and play in the 2012 World Series against the victorious San Francisco Giants.) As Gavin had said when we'd witnessed Felix Hernandez's perfect game in Seattle, we felt as if we were part of history.

We would feel even more connected to history when we visited the Henry Ford Museum the following day in nearby Dearborn. For me, this was one of the highlights of the trip, offering a window into the start of the modern age and the automobile's role in our nation's growth. I always enjoyed pointing out to Garon and Gavin people who'd started out with virtually nothing—Henry Ford was the son of a poor farmer— and accomplished great things, in part, because they lived in a land of opportunity.

As the person who invented mass-production techniques that made the automobile affordable for the middle class, Henry Ford opened up new vistas for people who'd previously spent most of their days within a few-mile radius. Ford, who lived from 1863 to 1947, was also a history buff and spent much of his life collecting historic artifacts.

The collection at the Henry Ford Museum—at over 250 acres, the largest indoor/outdoor museum in the country—includes presidential limousines, Thomas Edison's laboratory, the Wright brothers' bicycle shop, and the Illinois courthouse where Abraham Lincoln practiced law. We also took a bus to the Dearborn Truck Plant, where Ford has built vehicles for nearly a century, and watched as a truck was manufactured.

George Arredondo

From our hotel in downtown Detroit, we could see Windsor, Canada, and thought about taking a drive across the border, just to say we'd set foot in our neighbor to the north. However, after talking it over, as a family we decided that we wanted our journey to focus only on the United States—that was our story: fifty states in fifty weeks. No side trips to Canada needed.

However, concentrating on this side of the border didn't mean we ignored some obvious problems, and it was impossible to pretend that all was well when we were staying in downtown Detroit. It was not that I wanted to shock my sons by taking them for a walk through the blighted area where homeless people hung on to life and pleaded for money. I just wanted them to understand that not all people lived the way we had back in Northern California. America is a great nation, but it isn't perfect—and complex problems need everyone's attention.

Both boys were affected by the homeless people we saw in Detroit and wanted to know how these people had ended up this way. This was another "I don't have all the answers" moment, so when we got back to the hotel, we did some research, learning that the major reasons for homelessness are loss of a job, home foreclosure, divorce, devastating medical expenses, and untreated mental illness. Gavin said he wished he could do something for all homeless people and vowed to pray for them every night that they would remain safe and get the help they needed.

On September 29, we left Detroit and drove southwest for about three hours to Shipshewana, an Amish enclave in northern Indiana. While eating breakfast at an Amish-run restaurant called the Blue Gate, one of the locals filled us in on the town's mode of conduct. Since the Amish have renounced most modern conveniences, including automobiles and electricity, and believe in simple living, including dressing in modest clothing, it's considered rude to take their photos or try to engage them in English conversation since most speak a form of German.

While we were taking a traditional Amish buggy ride, Garon asked me if I knew why the Amish lived this way. I had to admit I didn't really know. Garon explained that it had to do with their form of Christianity and belief that they must eliminate pride and exhibit humility. When my hanging jaw showed that I was stunned he knew so much about this community, Gavin laughed and explained that he watched a reality TV series about the Amish. I guess since I'd been gone so much of the time for my job, I had no idea which television programs my sons were watching.

Next, we drove east for about thirty minutes to Elkhart and visited the RV/MH Museum (for the uninitiated, "MH" stands for motor home). When I pulled into the parking lot, a boy of about ten stuck his head out the window of an adjacent RV and said, "Mister, you got any kids in there?" I wondered why he was asking the question and hesitated before answering. "If you do," the boy said, "we'd sure like to play with them." Turned out, the friendly young man was one in a family of six kids traveling the country in an RV—and their goal was fifty states in fifty months (not weeks!). Garon and Gavin had a great time playing with the kids, and we enjoyed viewing some of the historic RVs on display at the museum. As Gavin would say, "We're part of history."

It was lucky that we encountered another family on a journey like ours because we could compare notes and share tips about campgrounds and other road-related issues. The meeting was good for another reason: It gave Garon and Gavin a chance to interact with other kids. Living and traveling in an RV can feel like total immersion in a pressure cooker; everything seems exaggerated, and emotions can run rampant. I sometimes felt guilty that Garon's method of slurping cereal drove me up the narrow walls of our humble abode. I realized, though, that I'd rarely been home for breakfast during most of Garon's life. How was he to know how his slurping affected me? Just as I'd had no one to teach me how to behave in social situations, I had been absent during much of the boys' childhood. I was just glad that I'd made a U-turn, and I had a chance to make up for lost time.

The next day, we drove about four hours east to Cleveland, Ohio, arriving in the Buckeye State. After we all admitted that we didn't know what a buckeye was, we learned via the Internet that it's a type of nut-bearing tree. When we arrived in Cleveland, it was rainy and cold, and it felt especially cold to us thin-blooded Californians. We took in an afternoon game at Progressive Field, where we froze in the upper deck and witnessed the Indians stampede the Kansas City Royals fifteen to three.

Even though we weren't used to cold, rainy Ohio, we decided to put on our hoodies and jackets and take a drive to Rocky Point, a rock formation with a gorgeous view of Lake Erie. When we arrived, the boys ran around near the lake and got their blood moving. They worked up an appetite for our dinner at Danny Boys, which won the prize for best bread (and we tasted a lot of bread) on the trip.

When we'd started this journey, I'd wondered if we'd gain weight, since we were spending a lot of time in the RV and eating out at restaurants. However, Melinda made a point to work out every morning and made sure the rest of us got a lot of exercise—walking, bike riding, and hiking. Coaxing us into activity was another of the myriad duties Melinda assumed throughout the day; lucky for us she is a master multitasker.

Fifty States, Fifty Weeks

The boys were diligent about keeping up to date with their school assignments and got some terrific educational opportunities in the places we visited. On October 1, we touched down at the Great Lakes Science Center in Cleveland, where we explored space and astronauts at the NASA Glenn Visitor Center, and then viewed a movie called *To the Arctic* at the Omnimax Theatre. The 3-D experience of the frozen tundra made Cleveland seem a whole lot warmer.

Melinda had done so much running that she had worn out her shoes, and Garon was growing so fast that he needed a bigger pair. We took a detour to the local mall for my wife and son to be outfitted with athletic shoes that would take them through the coming months. I hoped Garon's new shoes would last him a few months, but at the rate he was growing, you never know—we'd just have to find out.

CHAPTER 8

Expect the Unexpected

ON OCTOBER 2, we entered Pennsylvania, the Keystone State. Legend goes that it was so named because of its pivotal role in the fight for freedom during the Revolutionary War. We decided to stay in the Pittsburgh area—located near the state's southwestern corner—for a few days to explore this modern city on the banks of the Ohio River that over two million people call home.

We'd officially arrived in the Eastern United States, and I attributed the distinct East Coast feeling to the slant of autumn light, the brilliant fall colors, and the chill in the air. I felt an enormous sense of accomplishment that we'd made it from the Western United States to the Eastern United States, and I had complete faith that we would return to Whittier safe and sound.

From *How Not to RV*, I had learned not to over plan, and during the trip, I tried to follow that bit of guidance. However, I now understood that this dictum had a subcategory: *expect the unexpected*. Meaning that it was fine to wing it, but you had to prepare yourself, at least mentally, for any and all possibilities. This meant applying caution when necessary, such as leaving an RV camp that didn't feel safe, coping with changes in the weather (and learning to drive in the rain!), dealing with poor service and inedible meals, and, as much as possible, going with the flow.

I thought I'd prepared myself for just about anything that could happen, but that was before my encounter with something that, for us, turned Pittsburgh into an American version of horror-movie Tokyo, complete with unconquerable beasts invading our home. Yes, we experienced an alien invasion in the form of the ghastliest pest I have yet encountered: the stinkbug.

We had never before heard of the stinkbug, let alone seen one. However, we were plagued by these monsters from the moment we entered Pittsburgh until long after we'd left.

We first spotted these pests when we stepped out of our RV in the hotel parking lot, after we'd just celebrated our arrival in Pennsylvania with the ceremonial placing of the sticker on our US map. When we asked the concierge at the hotel, "What are those bugs outside?" we learned that these creepy crawlers are called "stinkbugs," and they come out when it is hot.

Wait a minute. It was October 2, and it didn't feel hot to us. Then again, the sensations of hot and cold are relative. Maybe it was hot for a stinkbug.

As soon as we checked into our room, I did an Internet search and learned that the stinkbug was accidentally introduced into the United States from Asia, hitching a ride in packing crates. The first US specimen was collected in Allentown, Pennsylvania, in 1998. Since then, the stinkbug has proliferated throughout much of the Northeast, and they are considered a major agricultural pest.

That night, when I took Garon to a Pittsburgh Pirates game at PNC Park, we saw stinkbugs everywhere. Nearly three-quarters of an inch long, with a brown, armor like shell, the stinkbug lives up to its name, emitting what's called a "cilantro-like" odor when disturbed. Stinkbugs were in the stands as we watched the Pirates beat the Atlanta Braves five to one. Melinda and Gavin had decided to stay at the hotel to catch up on schoolwork. After hearing how we were "bugged" at the stadium, they laughed, and I couldn't blame them.

The next day, Garon and I ventured to the ballpark for a daytime Pirates game, where the Braves rallied, shutting out the home team four to zero. Disappointed at the Pirates' loss, I imagined that the stinkbugs were emitting their unique form of protest—anyway, there was a spicy scent in the air, and it wasn't nachos.

George Arredondo

Gavin and Melinda were making terrific progress catching up on schoolwork. While they applied themselves to the "Three R's," plus a few more subjects, Garon and I attended a Boy Scout meeting with Troop 243 in Sewickley, Pennsylvania, where Scoutmaster Bob Smith traded a few patches with Garon, who filled in the Scouts about our trip. Garon is a terrific speaker and always manages to capture the audience's attention through his enthusiasm and confidence. Go Garon!

Since Melinda and Gavin had been cooped up for a few days, we decided on a family field trip to the Senator John Heinz History Center in downtown Pittsburgh. This huge and impressive facility—six floors of exhibits that tell the story of western Pennsylvania—honors H. John Heinz, a US senator and member of the Heinz family, manufacturer of a range of food products, including our favorite ketchup. Highlights included a visit to the "museum within the museum," the Western Pennsylvania Sports Museum, where we viewed a range of memorabilia related to baseball and other sports.

After touring the Heinz 57 exhibit—about the history of the H. J. Heinz Company—we were hungry for some ketchup-laden sandwiches and made our way to a local landmark, Primanti Bros., a Pittsburgh tradition since 1933. The mammoth sandwiches were like nothing we'd ever eaten before (or since!), with coleslaw and fries inside the bread. When we got back to the hotel, Garon worked off that calorie bomb with some spirited saxophone playing. The rest of us were content to sit back and listen to him play.

When we headed out of Pittsburgh the next day, the boys started to watch their homeschooling DVDs, but soon I heard a ruckus in the back of the RV. It sounded like someone slamming something against the table. Was it a student protest? An equipment malfunction? Then an odor wafted toward the front of the RV, and I knew the problem: stinkbugs.

I'd read on the Internet that stinkbugs invade homes during the fall—and adults can live for up to a year. The warmth inside a house causes them to become active, and they may fly around light fixtures or cling to windows when the sun is shining. Gavin hoped for schoolwork and homework while we tried to catch the bugs, but they were everywhere: drawers, closets, hampers, bellows, cereal boxes, shoes, socks, everywhere! There was no getting rid of them. It was like a plague from the Old Testament, something none of us would have ever expected. Of all the things we'd encountered on the trip so far—except for our day-one accident—stinkbugs were, by far, the most challenging.

Pittsburgh is a beautiful, interesting city and a great place to visit, but try to plan your trip for the spring before the stinkbugs wake up from their winter hibernation.

With each boy equipped with a flyswatter, the only homeschooling concession Melinda had made to the infestation, school was still in session, and we drove north to Erie, Pennsylvania, situated on the shore of Lake Erie, and then made our way to a campground at Presque Isle Bay. We were surprised to find a campground open during the fall and decided to put down anchor for what might be one of the last times we could until we reached the Southern states. Even though it was cold and rainy, the boys needed to let off some steam and get some exercise, so they rode their bikes in the downpour and got soaked. As I watched them, it occurred to me that, as Californians, they'd had little, if any, experience playing in the rain, and they really enjoyed splashing through the puddles and getting muddy. It was nice to see them get the chance to play like boys.

When I was Garon's age, my younger brother and I were running the rough streets of Los Angeles—with no direction, no discipline, and no bikes. We had to navigate through gang turfs, avoid being caught in our own brand of mischief, and just try to stay alive day by day. What a difference a generation makes. My sons seemed positively pampered compared to what my brother and I went through. I shuddered to think of what could have happened to my brother and me while roaming around with nothing to do but get into trouble. Today, I know that God had us in his hand and watched over us during all those difficult years. My brother became what

George Arredondo

we'd tried to evade in our teenage years: a police officer. He recently celebrated twenty-five years with the Los Angeles Police Department.

I wanted to do something special for Melinda to show her how much I appreciated her support, her enthusiasm, and all she was doing to make the trip a reality. She had assumed so much extra work and was living so far out of her comfort zone that I could never make it up to her. Melinda had mentioned that she was looking forward to seeing the fall colors in the Northeast—something we'd only viewed in photographs. My one thought was to get to New England by mid-October so Melinda could see the autumn colors at their peak. I just hoped we didn't run into too many unexpected situations that would slow us down.

On October 6, we rolled into New York—the Empire State and the nineteenth state on our journey. Colorful fall foliage abounded, but it was cold and rainy, which meant we couldn't fully appreciate the landscape. We were looking forward to a bright, beautiful day when the red, gold, and orange leaves glowed in the sunshine. We checked into a hotel in Buffalo, and the boys worked on their school assignments while we waited for the rain to stop.

I love to read, so rainy days were definitely a welcome break from driving for me. Before we left on the trip, I had loaded up on Kindle versions of books and audiobooks. I'd chosen nonfiction books, selecting subject matter that would dovetail with places we visited, such as US history and presidential biographies.

For me, one of the greatest things you can share with your children is your love of reading. My reading addiction started when I was about ten years old and started listening to Dodgers games on the transistor radio my brother David gave me as a birthday present. After listening to a game with commentary by the master Vin Scully, I wanted to know what the sportswriters had said about the game, especially about my favorite player, Steve Garvey. So I started buying the *Los Angeles Times* to read the sports section. After a while, I started to read other sections of the paper. After that, I started to pick up books and read them—and I've never looked back.

On October 7, the weather cooperated—a spectacular, sunny fall day in New York—and we headed about fifteen miles from Buffalo to one of the world's most iconic locations: Niagara Falls. Located at the US/Canada border on the Niagara River, which drains Lake Erie into Lake Ontario, these monumental waterfalls were formed when glaciers receded during the last Ice Age and water from the Great Lakes forged a path to the Atlantic Ocean.

After so many years of viewing Niagara Falls in photographs, seeing it in person felt surreal—it was hard to believe that we were really there. I felt speechless for a moment, with a lump in my throat and tears in my eyes. I understood why Niagara Falls was one of the great wonders of the world.

We were really here! We had traveled all the way across the country to arrive at this spot at this moment and witness this natural phenomenon up close and in person. I was filled with gratitude to God and filled with awe and wonder for God's creations.

We wanted to experience Niagara Falls in all of its glory, so we bought tickets for a boat ride in the *Maid of the Mist*, which is North America's oldest tourist attraction, established in 1846. Before stepping on board, we each received a blue rain poncho, which managed to keep us at least partially dry during the thirty-minute ride as the eighty-foot, six-hundred-passenger boat drove up to the base of the American Falls and the Canadian Horseshoe Falls. Water and rainbows surrounded us as we pounded through the river, getting soaked—and loving it—our voices muted by the roar of the falls.

When we got back to shore, we wanted more, so we bought tickets for the "Cave of the Winds" tour, advertised as a "thrilling walk on the wild side that allows you to soak up the experience." We took an elevator 175 feet down to the Niagara Gorge, slipped on yellow rain ponchos and special walking sandals, and then climbed a wooden walkway along the Niagara River to a location called the "Hurricane Deck," situated just a few feet from the rumbling falls. At this spot,

George Arredondo

Bridal Veil Falls (the third and final portion of Niagara Falls) creates conditions that simulate the rushing wind and rain of a tropical storm. This was an exciting and unique experience filled with thrills, chills, and fortunately, no spills.

Standing in the swirling water and pounding wind, I welcomed the experience almost as if it were a baptism of sorts, feeling much of the anxiety I'd been carrying with me wash away. I hadn't expected an experience like this when I'd started out this morning. It was an unexpected but welcome blessing.

I figured I'd never experience a real hurricane but was grateful I had the chance to understand what people on the Atlantic Coast experienced when hurricane season hit each fall. A few weeks later, I realized I had spoken too soon.

The next day, we drove for four hours due east—an amazing drive where we witnessed the glory of autumn in the lush countryside, with its stately trees and rolling hills—and arrived in Cooperstown. When we parked at the Cooperstown KOA RV park, it was chilly outside. We had a nice, cozy time sitting around the campfire that Garon made—displaying his exemplary Boy Scout skills, with Gavin helping by bringing branches to keep the fire roaring.

We got an early start the next morning, arriving at the National Baseball Hall of Fame when it opened at nine. This gave us a full eight hours to explore the exhibits and try to take in the museum's nearly forty thousand artifacts displayed throughout the extensive facility's three floors. Opened in 1939, the Hall of Fame's stated mission is to "preserve the sport's history, honor excellence within the game, and make the connection between the generations of people who enjoy baseball." We felt as if we were making a pilgrimage when we visited the Babe Ruth Room, where a variety of Ruth's uniforms and home-run bats were on display. Many of the items came directly from Babe Ruth—and the New York Yankees—who, in the 1930s, responded to the curators' request for memorabilia.

Fifty States, Fifty Weeks

It's impossible to do justice to this great American museum except to say, "Go there!" One experience at the museum was so unexpected that it nearly qualified as supernatural. At first, what I was looking at didn't really register. Was I misreading the signage? Could it really be true? I started to believe my eyes when Garon and Gavin started pointing, jumping up and down, and speaking at the same time. Yes, we were looking at the glove from Felix Hernandez's perfect game, the one we'd witnessed near the start of the trip in Seattle on August 15. How perfect was that? It was as if we had traveled from Seattle to Cooperstown, New York, along a parallel path with the glove.

I felt so filled with awe and wonder that I almost felt like kneeling to show my respect and gratitude for my creator. While driving, I had learned to read the signs, but Felix Hernandez's perfect-game baseball glove was the biggest sign I had yet viewed while traveling. It showed us that God was at our side and had been there every step of the way since the decision to take the trip through this miraculous sight in Cooperstown and would be with us all the way back to Whittier.

George Arredondo

The next day, we drove south for about four hours, reaching New York City via the iconic George Washington Bridge. After parking at an RV campground in New Jersey, we rented a car then drove to a nearby train station and hopped on the number four train into the Bronx—a wild ride, where throngs of people squeezed in and elbowed each other for space. We thought this would be an eye-opening experience for Garon and Gavin, far different from anything they'd known in sheltered Granite Bay, California.

We were excited about visiting Yankee Stadium, a huge, ultramodern ballpark that opened in 2009, and the mood was upbeat as the home team beat the Red Sox three to two. Yankee Stadium marked the eighteenth ballpark where the boys had attended games.

When I decided to expect the unexpected, I knew that some experiences would be challenging, such as the stinkbugs; others would be uplifting, like standing under Niagara Falls; and some would be miraculous, such as Felix Hernandez's perfect game; but I realized that some could be scary, especially when it came to unexpected road conditions.

The Oregon Coast seemed like a jaunt in the backyard compared to the roads leading from New Jersey to Connecticut, which were full of fast cars, twists, turns, and confusing highway signs. I thought I was handling every curve ball the roads had to offer, until I looked up and slammed on my brakes, sending the car behind us hurling into our rear with a *pow* and a crunch of bikes. When I got out of the RV, the man in the car behind us was upset—and I couldn't blame him—but I'd had no choice but to stop. I'd spotted an unexpected "13.5" listed as the clearance above the upcoming bridge, and I doubted the RV could clear it. My irate fellow driver pointed out that this road was for cars only and asked, with more than a bit of a New Jersey accent and attitude, "Didn't you see the sign?"

Turned out, I hadn't seen the "cars only" sign because a tree had obstructed it. The good part was that I had spotted the danger—albeit at the last minute—and had avoided slicing off the top of the RV. The bikes could be repaired, I had room to turn around, and I was able to placate the other driver, whose vehicle was undamaged.

Fifty States, Fifty Weeks

When we reached calm, quaint Connecticut, we felt as if we'd landed in a peaceful haven. After the frenetic pace of New York and New Jersey, we were ready for some quiet time and low-key activities. We checked into a hotel and rested up so we'd be ready to explore our twenty-first state—nicknamed the Constitution State because as an original colony in 1638, Connecticut had boasted the first constitution in the colonies' history.

The next morning, we bundled up in our warmest sweaters and jackets and headed off to Bristol to visit the headquarters of ESPN, the sports network where we obtained much of our baseball news. The network's campus resembles what you'd expect at a university, with lots of trees and grass, and inside there was plenty to see, with the sets for various television programs (such as *ESPN's Sports Center*), broadcasting booths, and murals of sporting events on the walls. The place was jumping with activity, but everybody seemed to be having a great time—and what sports fanatic wouldn't want to work at ESPN?

On the way to Bristol that morning, we'd passed through Newtown, Connecticut, and I later remarked to Melinda that I understood why people who worked in New York chose to live in Connecticut, telling her it looked like a great place to raise a family, a safe, tight-knit community that reminded me of Granite Bay, California. Two months later, I would remember these words.

The following day, we arrived in Hartford, the state capital, and were looking forward to exploring the Mark Twain Home, the rambling nineteen-room Victorian mansion where Twain lived from 1874–1891 and wrote many of his most beloved works, including the *Adventures of Huckleberry Finn*, considered by literary critics as one of the greatest books ever written. The site also includes a museum that features films and exhibits offering insight into the author, his work, and his legacy.

After the tour, I noticed something unexpected: a placard marked, "Sign up for the 2 p.m.–5 p.m. book-writing class." It was now 1:30 p.m. Could I really have spotted this opportunity while there was time to sign up? When I asked the person at the desk if seats were still available, she told me yes. It would probably be expensive though, right? When I learned that the fee was only forty dollars, I turned to Melinda and the boys and asked if they'd mind hanging out for a few hours in the RV. Melinda was happy that I wanted to take the class and glad to get Garon and Gavin back in school mode.

For the next three hours, I participated in the class, in which a half dozen people talked about the books they planned to write. Until I'd seen the sign at the Mark Twain House, I had only a vague idea about writing a book—I'd told the rude worker at the RV repair shop in Redding, California, that I intended to write one, but that may have been for show. What a blessing for the idea to crystallize in the home of one of America's greatest writers. When the author conducting the seminar asked what my book was about, I said without hesitation that I was traveling to all fifty states with my wife and sons and intended to tell the story of our adventures on the road.

The other authors were encouraging and enthusiastic, telling me, "We want to read that book!" Well, here it is—and I have Mark Twain to thank for the unexpected inspiration.

CHAPTER 9

Halfway Home

AFTER TEN WEEKS on the road, we were already nearly halfway home. The time and the miles had breezed by—and I couldn't help but draw a parallel between the trip and my own life. At age forty-eight, I was more than halfway through my expected lifespan, but unlike those who never consider their ultimate demise, I wasn't hesitant about thinking about my own mortality.

The way I looked at it, many people wasted precious time pursuing activities and possessions that didn't matter in the big scheme of things. These folks lived as if death would never catch them—and they chased the brass ring while shortchanging what really mattered: spirituality, family, and community. However, as the collective wisdom goes, on their deathbeds, people don't wish they'd spent more time at work.

Our journey across America was part of my personal bucket list, spending 24-7 with family members while sharing the wonders of America. I'm not implying that it was always easy—traveling is stressful under the best conditions—but it was always worth it.

In mid-October, we were in New England, enjoying the peak of a breathtaking autumn and surrounded by historic landmarks that commemorated our nation's fight for independence during the Revolutionary War. I thought of the sacrifices citizens had made for our freedom during this eight-year struggle, risking everything to establish the United States of America, and felt inspired by their example to create the kind of life I wanted for my family and myself. I was going to make sure the second half of my life was the best part of my journey on earth.

George Arredondo

Halfway through the trip, my major realization was the awe and appreciation I felt for my wife, understanding how blessed I was that God had brought the right partner into my life. Each day, I discovered something new to value about her—the patience she showed while working with Gavin on his school assignments, the way she encouraged Garon with his Scouting badges, how she maintained her health and fitness, and how she supported all of my dreams and plans.

I realized that for many years I had not been an equal partner but had served primarily as a breadwinner, which wasn't enough to contribute in a relationship. I vowed to bring more to our partnership and to our family life and to let Melinda know how much she meant to me.

When she remarked on the magnificent fall foliage in Vermont, I took the opportunity to segue into a compliment, saying, "Each day, I wake up to a spectacular vision when I open my eyes and see you." She thought I was joking and laughed, making me realize that even if you're willing to change overnight, you have to set the stage before other people can take you seriously.

As we explored the scenic routes in Vermont—Highway 9 and Highway 100—we all became caught up in the beauty of the setting: the vivid reds, golds, and oranges that surrounded us. When we stopped to take a closer look at the foliage, I would sometimes take Melinda's hand and take a romantic stroll while the boys enjoyed running and jumping through the landscape. Even though it was rainy and cold—and Melinda had the sniffles—our sprits remained high.

A highlight was a visit to Quechee Gorge, nicknamed Little Grand Canyon, where Garon and Gavin had a blast climbing trees and rocks and later enjoyed stacks of pancakes smothered in maple syrup.

I had made a point to reach Vermont when the colors were at their peak since I knew this was something Melinda wanted to experience. I felt so good about sharing this perfect place and time with her and the boys and considered myself truly blessed. More and more, I realized that this trip had, in many ways, saved my marriage and renewed my relationship with my sons.

Next, I planned to head for New Hampshire but saw a sign for the Calvin Coolidge State Historic Site in Plymouth Notch, Vermont, and decided to take the exit, which led to a winding twenty-five-mile stretch of scenic Highway 100.

When we finally arrived at the Coolidge Homestead, where our thirtieth president was born and raised, we learned that the site was closed for the season. On a hunch, I looked up the phone number and placed a call, explaining that we were at the halfway point in our trip across the country and we really wanted to tour the location. A friendly woman told me that we were in luck because a school group was visiting the following day, and we could join the gathering.

We had to decide whether it was worth spending another night in the area and traveling once again to Plymouth Notch but finally decided to do it so we could add this presidential birthplace to our list of places visited.

After spending the night at a two-hundred-year-old hotel called the Salt Ash Inn, fulfilling Gavin's desire to stay at a bed and breakfast, we headed back to the Coolidge Homestead, arriving in plenty of time to take part in the private tour. When I asked if the location included Coolidge's presidential library, I learned that the presidential library system had started with the thirty-first president, Herbert Hoover, who succeeded Coolidge in office.

I was so thankful that we'd decided to make this stop because from my perspective as a father, it turned out to be one of the most inspiring locations during the entire journey. As we toured the site where Calvin Coolidge had spent his youth, the guide explained the special relationship that "Silent Cal," as he was affectionately known, enjoyed with his father. Even as vice president of the United States—an office he assumed in 1921—Coolidge wrote to his father every day.

George Arredondo

Coolidge was home for a summer visit in August 1923 when a messenger delivered a telegram at midnight, informing the vice president that President Warren Harding had died and he should return to Washington, DC, to take the oath of office. As a local official, Coolidge's father insisted on administering the oath, and at 2:47 a.m. on August 3, 1923, he swore in his son John Calvin Coolidge Jr. as the thirtieth president of the United States.

I found this story so inspirational because it reminded me about my priorities and how, more than anything in life, I desired a close relationship with my family members. I wanted to be the kind of father my sons sought for advice, looked to for guidance, and counted on for love and support. This father/son bond trumped anything the business world could offer. I wanted to compensate for what I'd lacked growing up; I'd only come to a belated friendship with my father during the few years before his passing in 1998.

Later that afternoon, we entered our twenty-fourth state, New Hampshire—the Granite State, so named for its many rock quarries—and spent a fun day exploring the historic seaport of Portsmouth. The boys had impressed me with how well they were doing in their homeschooling assignments, and the New England leg of our trip offered many opportunities for extra credit in our visits to historic sites.

The next day, October 19, we arrived in Maine—the Pine Tree State—our twenty-fifth state and the official halfway mark on fifty states in fifty weeks. If we wanted the trip to last a year, we would definitely have to slow down.

As we spent time in Portland, near the state's southern border, celebrating with the local specialty, lobster rolls, people often remarked that they were surprised to see that Garon and Gavin weren't in school. When we explained about our trip and the boys' homeschooling, the kids heard the common refrain of "you're so lucky." I think they were starting to believe it. After a few cold and foggy days in the state, which included a ride on a fire truck, a tour of a train museum, and a trip to Scarborough Downs racetrack, we made our first right-hand turn since Seattle and prepared to head south, starting with several days in Massachusetts.

The highlight of the visit to Boston was an afternoon of paternal pride with my sons on the USS *Constitution*, launched in 1797, the oldest commissioned naval vessel still in service. While checking the official website for information, I'd learned that civilians could sign up for the privilege of lowering the ship's flag at sundown and was able to reserve this honor for Garon and Gavin. Talk about goose bumps, tears in the eyes, and a lump in the throat—I had a severe case of all three as I watched my sons, outfitted in their Scout uniforms, enact this sacred ritual to the sound of a naval officer playing "Taps" on the bugle. I'm sure that Calvin Coolidge's father couldn't have felt more pride in his son than I did in both of mine, especially since the vessel was celebrating the bicentennial of its significant role in the US victory in the War of 1812. Afterward, Gavin said, "We're part of history. Again."

The boys got a crash course in the War of Independence as we explored historic sites, including Boston Harbor, location of the Boston Tea Party, where, in 1773, citizens protested British taxation by dumping tons of tea into the Atlantic. These visits gave us the chance to discuss when people have the right and the duty to protest unfair treatment and how it takes courage to stand up to an oppressor.

A trip to Boston isn't complete without a stop at the John F. Kennedy Presidential Library—a magnificent facility that houses papers, photographs, and artifacts of our thirty-fifth president—and a tour of Fenway Park, the oldest ballpark in the United States, which was celebrating its centennial year.

However, I was most excited to take my family to visit Harvard University in Cambridge, where I'd completed a management course a year earlier. During the classes, one of our exercises was to write a letter that would serve as our ten-year plan of how to make the world a better place. My letter had included these ten-year goals: (1) become a better husband, (2) become a better father, (3) see Garon graduate from college, (4) travel to all fifty states and write a book about it, (5) write a book about how to make a difference in corporate America.

As we joined a tour group at the Harvard Commons, I felt pride that I'd taken courses at the country's first university but also awe that I was already making a concerted effort to become a better husband and father—plus we were more than halfway through the trip to all fifty states.

While the trip to the beautiful Harvard campus was a source of elation, rumblings about the impending hurricane put me in a more sober mood. Nobody seemed to know where and with how much force the storm would hit, so I needed to make a calculated guess about where to go next.

We completed our visit to the area with a stop at Plymouth Rock, where the Pilgrims landed in 1620 in their flight from England to avoid religious persecution. It was quite moving to stand on the spot where these hundred settlers had stepped off the *Mayflower* and entered the New World. In many ways, our trip in the RV was just such a journey from an old life to a new life, filled with adventure and many unknowns, including where Hurricane Sandy would hit.

I decided to head southeast to Cape Cod, where we were fortunate to find an RV park still open for business. The two days we spent in this pristine location were truly the calm before the storm—we had a wonderful time exploring our spectacular surroundings and understood why the area was a vacation destination for people all over the world.

By October 28, it was clear that we needed to pack up and head inland. I tried to maintain a stoic demeanor, but inside I was alarmed, though I did my best not to show it. I put on the "Captain George" hat, with one intention: leading my family to safety. I decided to head for Rhode Island.

Around this time, we started to get e-mails from friends and family members back home; they were worried for our welfare and wondering why we didn't just come home, if not permanently at least for Thanksgiving.

Fifty States, Fifty Weeks

It was a great relief to book a room in a hotel undergoing a renovation because I was able to park the RV between two large trailers so I didn't have to worry about the vehicle tipping over in the storm. Because the hotel was under construction, it was equipped with a backup generator and other fail-safe systems. Businesses and schools in the surrounding area were closed and the streets deserted—in some ways, it felt like the end of the world. However, again, I didn't want Melinda or the boys to know I was worried.

Hurricane Sandy hit on October 29, and the only good thing about this experience was that after it was over, we could say we'd survived it. Throughout this natural disaster, with the raging winds and torrential rains making it feel as if the hotel would blow away, I had faith that we would remain safe. After the hurricane's initial strike along the coast, the hotel started to fill up with more people seeking refuge—and, of course, the rates went up, up, up!

A few days later, the storm had abated, and we were able to leave the hotel for a visit to the famed Newport, Rhode Island, and celebrate Melinda's birthday with a walk along the coast, where a string of opulent mansions faced the water. This was where the scions of industry—the Vanderbilts, Rockefellers, and Astors—spent their summers in luxury. In addition, since it was Halloween, we took Gavin to the Providence Mall, where he went trick-or-treating dressed as a special-ops ninja. Now, if he could use his superpowers to keep that hurricane from blowing our way.

Coming from the state of California, where one day is pretty much like another, I now realized how much we took for granted since we didn't have to contend with weather extremes, except for an occasional earthquake. The weather had never really entered into my planning when I'd come up with the idea for the trip. The one exception was that I'd wanted to get to Alaska while it was still summer. However, in the end, how can you predict the weather? All you can do is deal with it once it's in front of you.

George Arredondo

We needed to move south—and, if possible, visit New York and New Jersey again before heading for Baltimore, where we planned to park the RV while we flew home for Thanksgiving. We had misgivings about breaking up our road trip, but the deciding factor was Melinda's mother, who was in poor health and asking daily for her daughter to come home. A visit to California would also give us the opportunity to take care of unfinished business in Northern California.

So, with some trepidation, we checked out of our cozy hotel and got back on the road, getting as far as Newburgh, New York, about forty-five miles from New York City. With no room at any inns in the area, we took advantage of a long-standing Walmart policy allowing RVs to park overnight in the lot. The store stayed open all night for people to shop and use the facilities. The kids had a great time shopping and touring the aisles at midnight.

The booked-up hotels were not just the result of Hurricane Sandy but also of the Army/Stanford football game at the United States Military Academy at West Point. We braved the cold, piling on layers of clothing, to watch the game.

As we made our way toward New York City, we saw one gas station after another closed for business—because no gas was available—and long lines at others. I was so grateful that we'd switched to a diesel-powered RV because that was the only type of gas readily available.

We decided to take a detour into Pennsylvania, where we checked into a hotel and were relieved to finally get showers. The little things in life really do make all the difference.

It was a real juggling act trying to figure out where to go and what to do next, checking the weather status, and calling the RV park in New Jersey to learn when it would reopen. I really utilized my management skills while planning this section of the trip.

Pennsylvania is filled with sites of historic interest, but what the boys wanted most was to visit the Hershey factory in Hershey, Pennsylvania, where our tour culminated in making chocolate bars. We also traveled to

Harrisburg, the state capital, and spent an afternoon at the National Civil War Museum. We were all learning so much on this trip, especially how cold it gets on the East Coast in November. Brrr!

Pennsylvania was the site of many Civil War battles, most notably the Battle of Gettysburg in July 1863, where nearly ten thousand perished, considered the turning point in the war. We spent a day touring the battlefields and cemetery, feeling gratitude for those who gave their lives to end slavery. We were so impressed with the well-preserved site—one of America's most esteemed landmarks—that the next day we returned for another visit.

At the Gettysburg National Cemetery, Gavin had many questions about the soldiers who'd lost their lives and talked about seeing them in heaven. We'd noticed that Gavin talked quite often about heaven, and it was starting to worry us a bit.

By November 9, we got the go-ahead to make our way to the RV park in New Jersey—finally open for business! However, when we arrived, what we saw was a parking lot filled with vehicles belonging to people working to repair damage caused by Hurricane Sandy. We couldn't wait to leave the next morning to book a hotel in Manhattan and take a bite out of the Big Apple.

We decided on a guided tour and were charmed by our proud-to-be-an-American tour guide, a man who hailed from South Africa. With visible pride, he pointed out New York City's iconic landmarks: the Statue of Liberty, the Empire State Building, Times Square, Wall Street, and much more. I'm a city guy and was looking forward to sharing the wonders of this metropolis with the boys, and, since both love architecture, they were suitably impressed by the concrete canyons. However, Gavin's favorite location was the world's biggest Toys "R" Us in Times Square, where we finished out the day under the neon signs of the Broadway District.

On November 11, we took the elevator up to the observation deck of the 102-story Empire State Building—the world's tallest building from its opening in 1931 until 1972. We spent time looking out over the city, where crews were busy trying to restore services and clean up the after-effects of the storm. There's nothing like a disaster to bring out the best in people. This hit home when we watched military veterans march in the Veterans Day parade. Observing brave Americans who'd defended our country in many wars during the past century filled me with a sense of pride in our nation and our citizens.

After three days in New York City, we arrived back at the RV park, where we were relieved to find that the RV was still there and in good shape. Since we had a few more days before we were flying out from Baltimore, I figured we should take a quick detour to Philadelphia, which had once been the nation's capital. In Philly, we visited Independence Hall, where the Declaration of Independence and the Constitution were signed. It was awe-inspiring to stand in the room where these precious documents began. We capped off our tour of the City of Brotherly Love with a visit to the Liberty Bell—a symbol of American independence that dates back to 1752.

Afterward, we made our way to Baltimore, spending a day catching up on laundry and schoolwork before flying to California on November 16, giving Melinda a week to spend with her mom before Thanksgiving.

After three and a half months on the road, visiting America's many treasures, I had a feeling that instead of natural wonders, our family members would be more interested in natural disasters, specifically: how had we survived Hurricane Sandy?

CHAPTER 10

Attitude of Gratitude

As it turned out, we were happy about taking a hiatus from our road trip during the Thanksgiving holiday. The visit reminded us how much we had to be grateful for, such as wonderful friends and loving family members, not to mention a home state with ideal weather and terrific sports teams. We made the most of our ten days in California by spending time with people who meant so much to us, and it was the first time we'd seen many of our extended family members in a long, long time. This reminded us why moving back to Southern California was a big positive; for Melinda and me, it meant close access to our sisters, brothers, and their children, plus our mothers, and for the boys, a chance to get to know their twenty cousins.

I was happy to spend these days visiting with my seven siblings: David, Yolanda, Patricia, Sandra, Lisa, Alex, and Sylvia—loving, hardworking people who care about their families and the community.

While we were in California, Melinda spent quality time with her mom at the assisted-living facility and often took the boys with her. Their grandmother kept remarking that she was amazed at how tall the boys were getting. Well, Grandma, with a mother who's five feet eight and a father who's six feet one, the kids can't help it.

On Thursday, November 22, we gathered at my sister Sandra's house for a Thanksgiving feast. As we sat down to break bread together, I felt so grateful to be in the warm circle of relatives. Melinda comes from a family of eleven children, and I hail from a family of eight kids, so whether we celebrate a holiday with her side of the family or mine, we are assured a lively, enthusiastic gathering.

I felt especially grateful that Garon and Gavin were getting to know their cousins, who would form a built-in set of Southern California friends when we returned from our trip. After spending most of their lives in Northern California, the boys would have to start over in a new school while making new friends. The cousins would help ease this transition, and I so appreciated their presence in my sons' lives.

As we filled up with turkey and all the trimmings, the people around the table wanted to know about our trip. They seemed amazed that we were really doing it, saying it seemed like something people only did in the movies or on TV. Melinda told me later that she enjoyed relaying incidents from our journey because it brought the trip into focus for her, making her recall sights, sounds, and other sensory details. However, as I'd suspected, our relatives were mainly interested in hearing about Hurricane Sandy, asking us to heap on more anecdotes as they heaped their plates with food. They offered their thanks that we'd made it through unharmed. Amen to that.

We filled our time in the Golden State, hanging out with friends and relations, taking in a few Lakers games, attending Scout meetings, and finding time to celebrate Gavin's tenth birthday on November 23. We marked the occasion with a trip to the Santa Monica Pier, where the boys enjoyed the rides, followed by a mini celebration with gifts and treats. We saved the major festivities for a few days later, when we drove to our old home base in Northern California and enjoyed a party at Laser Craze, where Gavin, along with his brother and friends, had a blast playing laser tag and arcade games.

During our visit to Northern California, we were able to take care of some remaining business issues and share time with our friends in the area. A highlight for Gavin was spending a few days with his Aunt Donnie—someone he not only idolized but also talked to every day while we were on the road. Now he could fill her in on all the details in person and enjoy some marathon sessions playing games with his Skylander action figures—legendary heroes and champions of Skyland.

George Arredondo

On Monday, November 26, Garon planned to make a presentation to his Scout troop for his life-badge board of review but woke up extremely ill, with body aches and chills. Despite feeling terrible, Garon was a trooper, showing up at the meeting and following through with his presentation. His efforts paid off, and he passed his BOR.

The next day, we drove back to Los Angeles, with Donnie accompanying us to Gavin's delight. During the ride home, both nephew and aunt had a great time sitting together, chatting, and playing games. When we arrived in Whittier, the first thing Melinda did was visit her mother at the assisted-living facility. As Melinda told me later, her mother asked her to stay home and not resume the trip. Melinda did her best to explain that she had to return to the road and that the trip would be over before her mother knew it.

On November 28, we flew back to Baltimore, and after a long day of traveling, we arrived at the hotel at ten at night. As soon as we had settled into our room, I rushed out to the garage to check the RV, which had been parked there for twelve days. I was relieved that the engine fired right up and we could get back on the road the following day.

However, the next day we were sidelined—not because of the RV but because we were exhausted from our detour to California, along with the airline travel and time changes. We spent the day resting up and getting the boys reacquainted with their schoolwork.

The next morning, we felt refreshed and were raring to go, so we rented a car and set out for a tour of some notable Baltimore spots, starting with the Baltimore & Ohio Railroad Museum, described as the "oldest and most comprehensive railroad collection in the world." While holed up in hotel rooms, waiting out Hurricane Sandy, the four of us had spent considerable time seated around the Monopoly board, playing epic games. Now here we were in a real-life version of a spot on the game board: B & O Railroad. We learned so much at this remarkable museum, including the vital role that the railroad has played in American history, such as the opening of the West and the North's victory in the Civil War.

Fifty States, Fifty Weeks

Our next stop was the Babe Ruth Birthplace Museum, which features a tiny upstairs room where the baseball great arrived while his mother was visiting her parents. Seeing Ruth's humble birthplace reminded me that many of my heroes started out with virtually nothing and achieved greatness through perseverance and hard work. I felt grateful to live in a country where you could find opportunities to achieve your dreams. I also felt a sense of camaraderie with Ruth because we shared the same first name—he was born George Herman Ruth Jr. on February 6, 1895. As it turned out, his birthplace was just a few blocks from Camden Yards, the home of the Baltimore Orioles.

My favorite Ruth quote is "I swing big with everything I've got. I hit big or miss big. I like to live as big as I can." These inspiring words articulated my reasons for fifty states in fifty weeks and are a wonderful reminder that you have to live your passion.

Once back on the East Coast, we had to readjust to colder weather. Our recent days in California had spoiled us with milder temperatures. Additionally, we still hadn't acclimated to the time change. We were going to bed late and getting up late—a schedule Melinda found unappealing.

However, even with a late start, we were out the door in time to visit Fort McHenry National Museum and Historic Shrine, famous as the inspiration for the "Star-Spangled Banner." In some ways, this location epitomized what our trip was all about: the American never-say-die spirit at its best. I'll admit I had chills and tears in my eyes as we toured the fort and listened to the story of how Francis Scott Key had witnessed the stalwart Americans raising the flag after a protracted battle with British ships during the War of 1812 and was inspired to pen the iconic words, "O, say can you see by the dawn's early light." I have sung these lyrics thousands of times, thanks to my attendance at baseball games and other sporting events.

Since these lyrics are so often mangled, I'd like to express my gratitude to our great nation by including the words to our national anthem here.

George Arredondo

O, say can you see by the dawn's early light,
What so proudly we hailed at the twilight's last gleaming?
Whose broad stripes and bright stars through the perilous fight,
O'er the ramparts we watched, were so gallantly streaming?
And the rockets' red glare, the bombs bursting in air,
Gave proof through the night that our flag was still there.
Oh, say does that star-spangled banner yet wave,
O'er the land of the free and the home of the brave?

We learned that "The Star-Spangled Banner," which includes three additional verses, started out as a poem entitled "Defence of Fort McHenry," with the words set to a popular tune of the day. Never have music and lyrics blended in greater harmony. The song became America's official national anthem in 1931 in a congressional resolution signed by President Herbert Hoover.

As I walked the grounds of historic Fort Henry, I remembered that it was December 1, exactly four months since we'd started our adventure. So much had happened in this period of time—summer had turned to fall, and fall was turning to winter—and we had experienced so many of our country's beautiful places and rich traditions, as well as so much of its inspiring history. I felt my heart fill with appreciation for this chance of a lifetime.

The next day, we hopped in the RV and made our way to state twenty-nine—West Virginia, the Mountain State—heading straight for Harper's Ferry National Historical Park. Located in three states—West Virginia, Virginia, and Maryland—the four-thousand-acre park includes the historic town of Harper's Ferry, West Virginia—famous as the site of protests against slavery before the Civil War—a powerful location where the Potomac and Shenandoah Rivers converge. In 1859, John Brown and fellow abolitionists stormed the national armory in Harper's Ferry, trying to start an armed slave revolt. The raid was unsuccessful, and John Brown was executed, but the raid remained a pivotal event, leading to the Civil War.

I felt so much respect and appreciation for John Brown, a heroic man who had the courage of his convictions and protested against powerful opposition—as the Bible says, "a voice crying in the wilderness"—and paid for his beliefs with his life. Learning about John Brown led us into a discussion about bullying and having the courage to stand up for what's right.

Even in the exclusive community where we'd lived for the boys' entire school careers, there were bullies in the mix—kids who were allowed to get away with harassing other students. Melinda and I reported the incidents, but the administrative wheels moved slowly to make any changes. As a teen, I'd experienced more than my share of bullying and had to devise a circuitous route home, going miles out of my way to avoid getting beat up or shaken down for my lunch money.

Moreover, let's not forget the corporate bullies that most of us have experienced during our working life—people who thrive on browbeating other employees into agreeing with their points of view. My way or the highway is their motto, and they stay on top by keeping other people down. So what happens when you disagree with these know-it-alls? Well, you might just have to hit the road and tour the country.

After a couple of days at a terrific KOA campground in West Virginia, we headed for Virginia, nicknamed "Mother to the Presidents" because it served as birthplace for eight US presidents. We settled into accommodations in Alexandria, Virginia, near Washington, DC, and then took the Metro train to Arlington National Cemetery.

We arrived at this hallowed site in time to witness the hourly changing of the guard, an elaborate ritual enacted by three members of the US Army's Third US Infantry Regiment. Around the clock, a sentinel guards the Tomb of the Unknown Soldier—a monument dedicated to American service members who died but whose bodies were never identified. As I witnessed the moving ceremony, I felt my heart fill with gratitude for those who gave their lives to defend our country and our freedoms.

Visiting Arlington National Cemetery is an emotional experience—more than six hundred acres of white gravestones that mark the final resting places of the thousands upon thousands of veterans of our nation's conflicts since the Civil War.

As we were standing before the eternal flame, paying our respects at the gravesite of our thirty-fifth president, John Fitzgerald Kennedy, Gavin started to talk about heaven, as he'd done when we visited Gettysburg, Pennsylvania. For a kid who'd just turned ten, he showed a lot of emotional depth. However, we wondered why he seemed to be preoccupied with the afterlife.

While walking back to the Metro, I talked to Gavin and tried to figure out what was on his mind. We chatted for a while about what we'd just witnessed at Arlington and previously at Gettysburg, and I realized that Gavin was such a caring person that he was actually worried about all the people buried in these locations. He wanted to make sure they were safe and happy in heaven.

I expressed my feelings about dying—that I'm not afraid of dying but prefer to spend my time focusing on living.

"Life comes down to what people say about you," I offered. "Meaning, how well you've lived your life and what you've contributed to the world."

I also mentioned—perhaps unwisely for such a sensitive boy—that he didn't have to worry about what would happen to his mother or me when we died because we already had arranged for our final resting place. When Gavin looked perplexed, I added that some people are buried at Arlington National Cemetery and others are buried at Gettysburg, but we'll be buried at Rose Hills in Whittier, California.

"This way," I said. "You and Garon won't have to worry about what to do with us."

"You're saying that you already have a spot picked out?" he asked.

"Picked out and paid for," I told him. "When we get home, we'll go there for a visit."

The conversation was getting so absurd that we burst out laughing, breaking any tension. Gavin has a great sense of humor and always finds a way to lighten up a situation.

Since we'd started the trip, my conversations with the boys and Melinda had taken on much more depth. We were together all the time and, most importantly, shared our meals together while sharing conversation, especially during dinner.

Our trip to Washington, DC, also included visits to the White House, the Washington Monument, the Capitol building, and the Smithsonian Air and Space Museum. We ended our day with dinner in Old Town Alexandria, a town dating back to 1749, and then strolling through the streets where George Washington had walked.

After my conversation about heaven with Gavin, I was more than a bit concerned when he woke up the next morning extremely ill with the stomach flu. We decided to stay at the hotel, and Garon helped a lot by doing all the laundry, even our sheets and blankets. Later, I drove him to a Scout meeting with Troop 61 in Washington, DC.

The following day, Gavin was still sick but had improved over the previous day, even doing a bit of schoolwork. While Gavin and Melinda stayed at the hotel, Garon and I ventured out to visit the Lincoln Memorial and the Smithsonian National Museum of American History—locations that made us feel even more pumped up and inspired about our trip across the country.

After two days in bed, Gavin had bounced back, and he was excited about getting out of the hotel and visiting Mount Vernon, George Washington's two-thousand-acre estate in nearby Fairfax County, Virginia. The impressive site features Washington's mansion and gardens, as well as several museums. After paying our respects at Washington's tomb, we made our way to the mansion, which served as Washington's country house.

George Arredondo

While the boys explored the gardens, Melinda and I stayed on the back veranda, sitting in period-style rocking chairs and taking in the sun setting over the Potomac River. I'd read that George and Martha Washington always ended a day at Mount Vernon by holding hands and watching the sunset. The great leader was quoted as saying that he was honored to serve as president of the United States but his greatest honor was serving as Martha's husband.

Inspired by the setting, I shared with Melinda that my father had named me after George Washington. My mother and grandmother had wanted to name me Felix Jr., but my father explained that our first president was his hero. My father's favorite boss was named George. I'd always felt grateful that he'd given me my name.

Melinda seemed surprised to learn this anecdote.

"Why didn't you ever tell me that before?" she asked.

"It never occurred to me," I said. Then I added, "The trip is bringing out stories in all of us."

We kept our eyes on the boys, who were having fun exploring and chasing each other, but were enjoying spending a few quiet moments alone.

The beautiful location and the approaching dusk created a romantic, otherworldly mood. I reached out and took Melinda's hand and said, "Over two hundred years ago, George Washington sat on this spot with his beloved wife, Martha."

Melinda nodded, and I could see she was trying to figure out where I was going with this.

"Of all the honors I've gained in life," I said, "my greatest honor is being married to you."

Melinda looked at me for a moment then replied, "Is that what George Washington said?"

"That's what I'm saying," I told her.

In response, she burst out laughing, making me realize that historic anecdotes and romantic pronouncements don't mix. Melinda could see I felt rather deflated and said it was sweet of me to say that.

Just then, the boys arrived, and I asked Garon to take a photo of Melinda and me with the Potomac behind us. When I looked at the photo on the camera, it appeared fine. We had captured this romantic moment between husband and wife. However, when I viewed the photo on my computer, I saw Gavin in the corner of the image—he'd photobombed our romantic moment.

Since it was two weeks before Christmas, as a nod to the season, we purchased a wreath for the RV. We were looking forward to reaching the warmer Southern states but first wanted to visit several significant sites in Virginia. After checking in to a hotel in Williamsburg, we spent the next few days exploring the area, starting with the Colonial National Historical Park at Jamestown, site of the first permanent English settlement in North America, established in 1607.

The Colonial National Historical Park at Jamestown also encompasses the colonial town of Williamsburg and the village of Yorktown, site of the last major battle during the Revolutionary War. We stopped at Moore House, where officers from both sides of the conflict negotiated the terms for the British Army's surrender on October 18, 1781.

When people tell me they'd like to explore our country but don't know where to begin, I tell them to start with the national parks. They're national parks for a reason; they're historic, significant, beautiful, and well maintained.

On December 13, we headed toward Virginia Beach and checked into a hotel right on the beach. How amazing was it that we had left our home on the West Coast and were now on the East Coast, on the shore of the Atlantic Ocean in one of the most beautiful locations in the country, a place we probably would have never visited if we hadn't taken this trip?

Even though it was chilly, we decided to spend some time on the beach. Standing next to Melinda while the boys built a sand castle, I felt so grateful to have a partner who believed in me and my dreams, a true helpmate, soul mate, and life mate. In addition, as I watched the boys collaborating on their sand structure, I felt so thankful to be the father of two amazing young men.

The following day, we were able to fulfill one of the items on Garon's bucket list when we took a drive through the Chesapeake Bay Bridge, known as one of the seven wonders of the modern world. Garon was captivated by the remarkable structure, and I wondered if he'd try to build a sand version during our next stop on the beach.

We enjoyed a holiday spectacular when we drove the three-mile stretch of holiday lights along the Virginia Beach Boardwalk. The festive light show really revved up our holiday spirit.

We completed our tour of the area with a visit the next day to Fort Story, an active military base that's the site of the Cape Henry Lighthouse, built in 1781, the first lighthouse authorized by Congress. As we gazed up at this tall, white edifice, it became a symbol to me of America, shining the light of freedom throughout the world. I felt very, very grateful to live in such a place.

CHAPTER 11

Determi-NATION

DURING OUR MONTHS traveling across America, we learned about many amazing Americans who had made the world a better place through their courage, passion, and talent. As I drove the highways and byways, with lots of time to ponder, I realized that determination was the hallmark of these heroic individuals. They didn't give up and kept moving, even if it was inch by inch, toward their dreams and goals.

One of my favorite sayings is "there has to be a will behind the want." If you want to achieve something, you have to be willing to work for it, which sort of sums up our trip across the country and why we were on the road rather than sitting at home, talking about taking a trip.

While inventors and scientists understand that it may take hundreds or thousands of experiments before they achieve results, many people don't realize that the same principle holds true in everyday life. We need to act on our dreams, try things, and see what happens. Our experiments in life provide information about what we like and what we don't like, what works and what doesn't work—and show us how to adjust our will to our wants.

As we traveled during the month of December, my mind was often occupied with meditations about life, pondering the big questions. What is success? What is happiness? What is love? What is courage? What is good? What is evil? What is life all about?

However, while my thoughts were focused on lofty ideas and ideals, Gavin was thinking about more immediate concerns—specifically: How is Santa going to find us if we're not at home? He was counting on particular gifts and didn't want to take the chance of missing them.

Christmas was about a week away, and we hadn't decided where to spend that particular day. I figured it would relieve Gavin's mind if he could write a letter to Santa, listing our Christmas location while on the road. Even though I'd vowed not to over plan, it was time to make an exception.

Melinda and I advised Gavin to write to Santa, stating that we were traveling across the country and would be in Stone Mountain, Georgia, on Christmas Eve and Christmas. In a PS, Gavin promised to put out chocolate milk and cookies. We mailed the letter care of the North Pole. As soon as we posted the envelope, Gavin said, "You know, if Santa can't find me and gives my presents to another kid who needs them, that's OK too." We are so proud that this wonderful, caring person is our son.

Afterward, I thought about how determined Gavin had been to make sure Santa knew his whereabouts. As soon as he'd done everything in his power to send a message, Gavin seemed at peace with whatever happened. This reminded me that success isn't the goal; instead, the objective is to try with all your might to show determination.

On December 16, we entered state thirty-one—North Carolina, the Old North State—and the following day, we visited the Wright Brothers National Memorial in Kitty Hawk. Our trip had been filled with coincidences, and this was another: we arrived on the anniversary of the first powered flight, which occurred on December 17, 1903.

George Arredondo

Run by the National Park Service, the site, located in an area called the Outer Banks, is a tribute to two men's determination to make their dreams of flight a reality. Garon and Gavin had fun racing down the runways to see if they could beat the time clocked by the Wright brothers' plane and celebrated when they bested one of the flights.

Since this was an anniversary, the day included many visiting officials and formal celebrations, where we learned that the Wright brothers had selected this spot for its wind gusts and sandbanks, which would cushion the fall if they crashed. These American heroes—self-taught engineers from Dayton, Ohio—struggled for four years, braving difficult conditions, conducting experiment after experiment, until they took flight and changed the world. They held on, kept going, despite the naysayers, despite the people who said, "If God had wanted us to fly, he would have given us wings." Well, what about making our own wings? What about giving flight to our own dreams?

I felt kinship with Orville and Wilbur Wright and could feel their spirits bolstering me as we explored the area where they had lived and worked for years. Their heroism in the face of hardship gave me courage to keep pursing my dreams and trust that I was on the right path. I truly believe that if anything is worth doing, you'll find a way to do it.

The following day, we made our way to Raleigh, the capital of North Carolina, and checked into a Residence Inn, where Garon was ecstatic to have the upstairs suite all to himself.

In North Carolina, we felt the "Southernism" of the state; the mood, food, accents, and pace had a marked difference. Before starting out on the trip, people had advised us to avoid the South because, as a Mexican American family, we might encounter prejudice. All these fears were unfounded. While Southerners may have given us long looks—out of curiosity, I believe—the people afforded us the same courtesies as they did everyone else.

On our first day in Raleigh, we visited the Marbles Kids Museum, a fun spot with many engaging interactive exhibits, and then stopped at the home where Andrew Johnson, America's seventeenth president, was born in 1808.

The Raleigh area is home to many college sports teams, and one of Garon's goals during our trip was to see Stanford play, since he'd attended an academic program at the university the previous summer. The two of us enjoyed a night out together to watch the Stanford basketball team play North Carolina State. Stanford was the favorite, but the game ended in an upset, North Carolina winning eighty-eight to seventy-nine.

While parked at RV camps, we played a lot of basketball, with the boys teaming up to beat their dad. When the trip started, the brothers argued with each other, but soon they realized they had to learn how to play together, including running plays and practicing before games. Soon enough, the duo started to best their old man.

On December 19, Gavin and I were looking forward to some one-on-one time at a local sporting event. I'd promised to take him to watch Duke University's basketball team, but, with Duke at ten and oh, I couldn't get tickets for the "winningest" team in college basketball. I let Gavin feel bummed out for a couple of seconds then asked, "Do you think I'm going to give up that easily? Come on. Let's go."

We drove to nearby Duke University and made our way to Cameron Indoor Stadium, one of the oldest arenas in the country. I told Gavin to watch and I'd show him how to get tickets to a sold-out game. As people approached to enter the arena, I held up two fingers in what looked like a peace sign, but the gesture really meant I wanted to purchase two tickets. We stood there for what seemed like forever, with Gavin growing more disappointed with each passing minute. I told him that if you really, really wanted something, you had to keep trying. I kept standing there with my two fingers raised.

People are skeptical about selling their extra tickets to strangers, concerned that the buyer might be a scalper, out to resell the seats for exorbitant prices, and if you're not a scalper, the ticket holders might not want to sit next to someone they don't know.

George Arredondo

After about an hour, a man approached and said he had two tickets—first making sure we weren't going to resell them—and allowed me to snag two seats for the regular price. Gavin was elated and looked at me as if I were his hero. See what persistence can do!

We had open-admission tickets—meaning no assigned seating—where the holders were seated in various spots to fill gaps in the audience. Gavin and I got the best seats in the house: front row in the student section, where we had to promise to participate in the chants, songs, and voodoo signs against the opposition (Cornell), as well as make faces, clap, jump, and pound our feet. It was the wildest two hours we'd ever spent at a basketball game. Duke won the contest, to Gavin's delight.

Fifty States, Fifty Weeks

On the drive back to the hotel, Gavin said, "Thanks for taking me to my first Duke game, Dad. It was really easy getting good seats." Then he smiled and said, "Only kidding. You did a great job getting seats."

We were both beat from all the energy we'd expended during the game, exhausted and wiped out but happy. We'd been fully engaged in getting the tickets and participating in the game. It was one of the highlights of the trip for Gavin and me.

While pulling out of a parking lot the following day, our bike rack snapped as I drove over a speed bump, sending our bikes spilling onto the ground. We couldn't repair the bike rack and decided to leave our bikes behind, with a sign that said, "Free." Five days before Christmas, a couple of people got the bikes they'd been hoping for.

We checked into an RV park in Hamer, South Carolina, and had dinner at a Mexican restaurant, part of an entertainment complex called South of the Border, meaning south of the North Carolina border. It was fun to hear how Alan Schafer had opened the spot over fifty years before. It started as a beer stand and evolved into a tourist attraction, a combination of Old South and Old Mexico.

That night, the RV rocked and rolled in a torrential rainstorm, complete with high winds. The extreme weather in the Midwest, East, and South were new experiences for us. We didn't get much sleep that night.

The following morning, it was still storming, but we headed toward Georgia, our thirty-third state, because Gavin wanted to make sure we were settled in Stone Mountain by Christmas Eve so Santa could find us. Our first stop in the Peach State was Augusta, where we had lunch at a Mexican restaurant and learned that someone had paid our bill in a random act of kindness. Now that's Southern hospitality!

The rain cleared up, so I suggested we make a quick stop at the Augusta National Golf Club, home to the Masters Tournament. I just had to have a picture of myself at this world-famous course! I'd started playing golf as a young man, my interest in the game having been sparked by watching Lee Trevino on television. On Sundays, my dad's one day off, he'd watch sports on TV and never missed a golf tournament that featured Lee Trevino, an icon to the Mexican-American community. From an impoverished background, Trevino rose through sheer persistence to become one of the greatest all-time golfers. For this and so much more, Trevino is one of my heroes.

While in Augusta, we visited the childhood home of America's twenty-eighth president, Thomas Woodrow Wilson. Young Tommy lived in Augusta for ten years while his father was the local Presbyterian minister. Born in 1856, Wilson resided in the area during and immediately following the American Civil War (1861–1865), which had a profound influence on him: as president, he attempted to find peaceful solutions to conflicts, including helping to establish the League of Nations.

Before the trip, many of our presidents were just names in a history book, and I had only vague ideas of when many had lived and what they had accomplished. Our journey introduced us to the men behind the names, people whose stories varied but in one way resonated: they were all determined to make a difference in the world.

On to the important issue of the day: getting to Stone Mountain Park, which we reached on December 23, to Gavin's relief. We were staying in Southern comfort at the Stone Mountain Inn, a majestic plantation-style hotel. The holiday season was in full swing at the Stone Mountain Park Christmas Celebration, an extravaganza of yuletide lights, entertainment, and decorations, including a parade and fireworks. Melinda and the boys were pleased with the location, saying it was the perfect place to spend Christmas.

Fifty States, Fifty Weeks

These elaborate festivities made me think of my own upbringing, which was a complete contrast, where holidays and birthdays were only noted in passing but not really celebrated. My parents were just too overworked and overextended to even try to make any day special, telling us that we were lucky we had a roof over our heads and food on the table. With my sons, I didn't want to overcompensate for the things I missed growing up, so I tried not to go overboard, but I admit I did so at times. I enjoyed the holidays as much as Garon and Gavin did.

On Christmas Eve, we split up for separate activities. Melinda went for a walk, Garon and Gavin visited the nearby rock quarry (the largest in the United States and the source of granite used in many of our national monuments), and I shopped for a Christmas tree. After dinner, we decorated the tree and watched *Santa Claus Is Coming to Town*. When the movie was over, Gavin set out cookies and chocolate milk for Santa and then headed off to bed. He was so excited to see if Santa would find him. Garon had the holiday spirit too, and he was hoping for some special gifts. Well, Santa didn't disappoint. He showed up at our hotel and left a sack full of gifts for Gavin and Garon.

As soon as he woke up, Gavin was jumping up and down with excitement. He'd received everything he'd asked for and more, and so did Garon. After breakfast, Melinda took a run around Stone Mountain Park while listening to Pastor T. D. Jakes on her iPod. We were looking forward to visiting Pastor Jakes's church in Dallas. While Melinda went for a run, the boys and I watched a Lakers game on TV. Overall, it was a relaxing and fun Christmas.

Before leaving the area the following day, we viewed the Confederate Memorial Carving—at ninety feet high and one hundred and ninety feet wide, the largest high relief sculpture in the world—carved on the side of Stone Mountain and depicting three Confederate leaders from the Civil War: General Robert E. Lee, President Jefferson Davis, and General Thomas "Stonewall" Jackson. Nearly sixty years in the making, this carving not only runs deep into the mountain face but also shows that sentiments about Old Dixie run deep and exhibits the determination of the people who planned, funded, and executed the artwork.

While viewing this carving, the boys wanted to know why these three men were celebrated in this way and what they'd done to deserve the honor. This led us into a discussion of what the Civil War was and why the North and South fought this four-year conflict. I thank the three Southerners depicted on the mountain for facilitating our first real discussion about civil rights, and we managed to conduct this deep discussion while shivering in forty-degree temperatures. Before leaving the area, Garon and I took a ride on a ski lift called the Summit Skyride to the top of Stone Mountain, where we were able to see all the way to Tennessee—our next destination.

Two days after Christmas, we were on our way to Chattanooga, Tennessee, the Volunteer State, with Gavin placing the sticker on our map.

This gorgeous spot near the Georgia border offered a variety of attractions: Ruby Falls, the nation's largest and deepest waterfall; Lookout Mountain, which offers a spectacular view of six states; and the Incline Railway, which took us on a steep ride one mile up the face of the mountain.

Mountains had featured in our surroundings for the past few days, and I couldn't help but grasp the metaphor—you don't climb a mountain or do anything significant with one or two steps but by steady application and persistence. In a sense, our trip was like climbing a mountain, each state we visited taking us closer to the peak.

On December 29, we arrived in Birmingham, Alabama, with the temperature below freezing, around thirty degrees. None of us had ever experienced weather this cold; we couldn't get used to it and didn't want to. We were really going to appreciate California's temperate climate when we returned.

On Sunday, December 30, we worshipped at the 16th Street First Baptist Church, and we were moved as Reverend Price delivered an inspiring message called "A New Year, a New You." He advised everyone to forget the past, focus on the present, and press toward the future.

Because of its activism in the civil rights movement, the 16th Street First Baptist Church was the site of a racially motivated bombing on September 15, 1963, when four young girls were killed. Many believe this marked the turning point in the civil rights movement.

Later, we toured the nearby Civil Rights Institute and viewed exhibits, displays, and videos depicting the fight for equality. I noticed that Gavin seemed shocked and upset at some of the videos that documented conflicts between law enforcement and protestors during these difficult years. When I took him aside, Gavin said, "I'm good on the civil rights movement," meaning he'd seen enough. While I commiserated with Gavin, I also offered my thoughts on the matter, agreeing that these images were upsetting but explaining that people needed to look at this history to prevent future discrimination.

We spent New Year's Eve at a hotel in Atlanta. It was a pretty normal day. The boys did their schoolwork, and later Mel and I went to see a movie while Garon kept an eye on Gavin. We didn't get much sleep that night because revelers kept coming in and out of the hotel.

January 1 marked the fifth month on our journey across America. We decided to have a fun day at one of Atlanta's most famous institutions: the World of Coca-Cola, a museum dedicated to the world's best-known beverage brand. It's amazing to think that Coca-Cola, a Fortune-100 corporation, had such humble origins. In 1886, after many experiments, Atlanta pharmacist Dr. John S. Pemberton created a formula for a unique soft drink that drugstores could sell at soda fountains. During our visit, we stood in the vault where the Coca-Cola Company stores the formula—one of the most valuable pieces of business intelligence in the world. At the end of the tour, we visited the tasting room, where we sampled different versions of Coke. Bottlers adapt the formula, depending on the country's taste, and send Coke all over the world. Garon boasted that he tried sixty different varieties. With all that caffeine, we guessed he wouldn't get much sleep tonight.

We celebrated the new year with lunch at The Varsity, the world's largest drive-in, where, since 1928, customers have been greeted with, "What'll ya have?" We had great burgers, fries, and a local concoction called the Frosted Orange—a delicious orange-flavored shake. We finished the day with a tour of CNN, our favorite place for news.

On our last day in Atlanta, we paid our respects to Dr. Martin Luther King Jr. by heading to the Martin Luther King Jr. National Historic Site. The site features a museum that explores the lives of Dr. and Mrs. King, the home where Dr. King was born and lived for the first twelve years of his life, and the tombs of Dr. and Mrs. King, surrounded by a reflecting pool and an eternal flame. I think Gavin was happy that he didn't have to view any upsetting videos and instead could focus on King's inspiring messages, including his "I Have a Dream" speech. We also visited Ebenezer Baptist Church, where Martin Luther King Jr., his father, and grandfather served as preachers.

Our trip to Atlanta was completed with a visit to the Jimmy Carter Presidential Library and Museum, which honors our thirty-ninth president.

Fifty States, Fifty Weeks

Carter is an inspirational figure who, in many ways, accomplished more after his presidency than during his one term in office. He was determined to keep serving our nation and the world, and he has done so admirably.

Before leaving Atlanta, Garon and Gavin dropped by the Atlanta Area Council Boy Scouts of America office and received several patches for telling their story of fifty states in fifty weeks. In addition, we couldn't end our visit without a tour of Turner Field, home of the Atlanta Braves.

Our last stop in Georgia was the state's first city, the beautiful seaport Savannah, established in 1733. The British General James Oglethorpe named the colony after King George II—and, of course, I loved learning about more renowned Georges.

We checked into an RV park called the Red Gates, at one time an encampment for Confederate soldiers and later occupied by Union General Sherman after his March to the Sea during the Civil War. Savannah is truly the Old South, going back to the colonial era and bearing many reminders of the War Between the States. We took a trolley tour of the town, and Melinda fell in love with the city—a place of great charm, thanks to the antebellum mansions, magnolia trees, and cobblestone streets.

A visit to Savannah wouldn't be complete without a stop at the world-famous The Lady & Sons restaurant, owned by celebrity chef Paula Deen and her sons. The food exceeded our expectations, and we all dived into a feast of fried chicken (the best of the trip!), greens, and cornbread, with a healthy portion of Gavin's favorite, mac and cheese, which he rated the nation's best.

This wonderful meal reminded me of the bounty that is America, a rich table of gifts: freedom, opportunity, democracy, and so much more. I gave thanks that I was alive on this day, with my amazing family, traveling this glorious country—and I was determined to never forget for a moment how lucky I was.

CHAPTER 12

Sunshine State of Mind

IN THE PAST few weeks, I'd become aware of a habit I'd developed during the trip: I had become fixated on the monitor situated where a rearview mirror would appear in a car that displayed images from the vehicle's backup camera. I caught myself looking at the screen even when I wasn't backing up the vehicle. One day I realized that this behavior was giving me a clue that I was still fixated on the past and my previous job.

Nearly every time I checked the monitor, my thoughts would revert to the past and the decision I'd made about leaving my employment and driving across the country. I asked myself, *Was it the right decision? Would we adapt to a different environment and lifestyle? How would the boys adjust to school? How long would it take me to find a job? What if we ran out of money?*

Then one day, I became aware that I kept checking the backup monitor. I'd been doing this for months, and it had become a habit—so much of a habit that I wasn't even aware that I was doing it. I connected the dots between this repetitive behavior and my focus on the past rather than the road ahead. This insight helped me break a nonproductive habit and move forward.

Now we were moving toward Florida, the Sunshine State, for a few weeks of fun in the sun before taking the left turn toward home. We arrived in Jacksonville—a city on the Atlantic named for Andrew Jackson, seventh president of the United States—on January 5, the sixteenth anniversary of the day Melinda and I got married. Garon and Melinda cooked a spaghetti dinner to celebrate the occasion.

We all felt better in a warmer climate—hello, T-shirts!—and asked the boys to finish their schoolwork by one in the afternoon so we could get outside for some of that famous Florida sunshine. We hit the pristine Ponte Vedra Beach but also found time for some cultural activities, including a visit to the Museum of Science and History, where we watched some inspiring films about space exploration. Hey, that was the new me, focused on the future and the space in front of the RV!

On January 9, we headed south to Saint Augustine, the oldest continuously occupied settlement in the continental United States, founded by Spanish Admiral Pedro Menéndez de Avilés in 1565. We checked into the Bryn Mawr Ocean Resort, situated right next to the beach. The RV actually backed onto the sand, and we could hear the peaceful sounds of the waves during the night. Of all the places we camped, this was by far my favorite—spectacular location and remarkable view, and the weather was great too.

If I still had any doubts about the decision I'd made to leave my job, they melted away in the Florida sunshine as I opened the RV door and faced our ocean view. It was January, and other people were struggling in freezing temperatures, in snow, and on icy roads. Here I was in a T-shirt, in an RV parked on the beach. How lucky can you get?

I got up early to watch the sunrise over the ocean—a spectacular sight—realizing that I'd spent most of my life watching the sun go down over the Pacific. Watching the sun come up reinforced my resolve to focus on the present and future. I felt so blessed to witness the glory of God's creation during these sunrises on the Saint Augustine beach.

When we managed to tear ourselves away from our ideal RV campground, we visited several local attractions. As an avid golfer—and the boys were getting the bug too—we had to stop at the World Golf Hall of Fame, which features a real-grass, championship eighteen-hole putting course. We all took shots, but Gavin, dressed in his Lakers uniform, was the winner.

At the World Golf Hall of Fame, we also attempted the challenge hole, a 135-foot drive to an island green. After the boys took their shots, it was my turn. This was the most pressure I'd felt on the trip because I'd always presented myself to my sons as a good golfer.

I couldn't focus on my past golf triumphs but had to analyze the prevailing conditions and plot my strategy. A stiff wind and the surrounding water made the shot extremely challenging. Instead of a seven or eight iron, I used a six iron. I had to shoot on faith and hit where I couldn't see the green. I hit the ball and watched as the wind carried it right where I wanted it. The kids were so proud of me, jumping up and down and screaming. Even Melinda had to shout and stomp. In all humility, I'll say it was as perfect a shot as I've ever hit. When it was all over and I received my award—a commemorative poster—I told Gavin and Garon, "It's all a matter of practice."

Back at the campsite, which everyone adored, we had fun cooking out and playing football, baseball, and tag on the beach. This was living! Our days in Saint Augustine were, in many ways, the best of the trip—perfect location, ideal weather, and lots of relaxation and togetherness.

Before leaving the area, we visited old Saint Augustine and added another historic lighthouse to our list—the Saint Augustine Light, built in 1874 and still active—and toured the Castillo de San Marcos National Monument, a Spanish fort that dates from the late sixteen hundreds.

On January 11, we arrived in Orlando. A few years before, we'd visited Disney World, so we decided that we'd focus on other attractions during this trip. We gave the boys a break from school and enjoyed a whirlwind of activities, including visits to the Ringling Brothers and Barnum & Bailey Circus, Gatorland, SeaWorld, Legoland (Gavin's favorite theme park), and WonderWorks, where I was brought onstage during a magic act.

On day 175 of our trip, we made our way to the Kennedy Space Center and enjoyed participating in a group lunch with Astronaut Jerry Carr, commander of *Skylab 4*, who, it so happened, graduated from USC (a fellow Trojan!). In my current mode, where I had turned off the backup camera, I was particularly caught up in the astronaut's luncheon talk about how he prepared to go into space. Someday, I hoped to give talks about how I prepared to hit the road in my RV. As they say, everything is relative!

On January 18, we headed north to Madison, Florida, and checked into a Yogi Bear RV campground, inaugurating the location with a campfire and s'mores. The boys really enjoy the kid-friendly Yogi Bear sites.

The next day, we drove to Pensacola, the westernmost city in the Florida panhandle, located on the Gulf of Mexico, making our final left turn toward our final destination. While in Pensacola, we visited the National Naval Aviation Museum, the home turf of the US Navy flight demonstration squadron, the Blue Angels, which are garrisoned nearby. This remarkable museum, devoted to the history of naval aviation, with more than 150 aircraft and spacecraft on display, was a great bookend to our recent tour of the Wright Brothers National Monument in North Carolina.

With so many encounters with flight during the past few weeks, I felt empowered to face the future and ready for what it had to offer!

CHAPTER 13

Endurance

DURING LATE JANUARY and early February, we encountered people and places that had faced unimaginable hardships yet rose from adversity and demonstrated the spirit that built this country and that continues to make it great. What an inspiration!

When we left Florida, our first stop was Mobile, Alabama, a seaport city on the Gulf of Mexico, hard hit in 2005 when Hurricane Katrina struck and hit again five years later during the BP oil spill, the largest marine oil spill in the history of the petroleum industry.

People from Mobile exhibit the can-do American spirit in all its glory. When the USS *Alabama* (BB-60), which served in the Atlantic and Pacific during WWII, was retired in 1962, the people of Mobile saved "The Mighty A" from the scrap pile by raising $1 million to purchase the ship from the US government and create a tourist destination called Battleship Memorial Park. During Hurricane Katrina, the ship sustained $4 million in damage, with most repairs completed within six months.

As we toured the USS *Alabama*—including viewing the inside of the main gun turrets and antiaircraft guns—I thought of my father, who had joined the navy at age seventeen, spending four years in the Pacific on the USS *Ranger* (CV-61), a ship similar in size to the USS *Alabama*. Decommissioned in 1993, my dad's ship is in dry dock in Washington State, and since private citizens weren't able to raise enough money to save the vessel, the government plans to scrap the *Ranger*.

Touring the USS *Alabama* gave me a greater appreciation for people who serve on ships, including my father, spending month after month at sea in close quarters under difficult conditions. My dad told us there were more sailors than cots, and the men would have to sleep in shifts. Now that's tight quarters.

I felt proud showing the boys around the USS *Alabama*, telling them how their grandfather Felix, whom they'd never met, had faithfully served our country. On this day, I felt very proud of my father and hoped that pride rubbed off on my sons.

While in Mobile, we had to pay our respects by visiting the childhood home of baseball great Hank Aaron. With a career that spanned twenty-two years (1954–1976), Aaron was the only MLB player to hit thirty or more home runs in a season at least fifteen times. Aaron's childhood home, which he helped his father build with scrap lumber, has been relocated, and it now sits at the entrance to Hank Aaron Stadium in Mobile. Growing up so poor that he practiced playing baseball with bottle caps and sticks, Aaron endured poverty and racial discrimination—relegated at first to the Negro Leagues because of MLB's favoritism toward white players—to become one of the greatest players in baseball history, the player who, in 1974, broke Babe Ruth's home-run record.

On January 22, we entered Mississippi—the Magnolia State—and made our way to Gulfport, another city that sustained devastating damage during Hurricane Katrina and the BP oil spill. During Hurricane Katrina, our hotel, the Courtyard Marriott, was deluged with water up to the third floor, and the hotel now featured a line on the wall to mark the event.

I understood that people in Gulfport had made many sacrifices to rebuild their lives and continue to live in the area, as had all those on the Gulf Coast. They had to start over, make do with less, and in many cases find new ways to make a living. This especially applied to people who worked in hotels and restaurants, many of which closed and never reopened, and people engaged in the fishing industry.

I thought about our situation, how we were starting over in a scaled-down lifestyle with no immediate source of employment. In our case, it was a matter of choice, but the people on the Gulf Coast didn't have a choice. They just woke up one morning, and their whole world had changed. My heart really went out to them.

George Arredondo

The boys and I love to fish, so I thought a fishing excursion would give us an opportunity to learn how the area was recovering from Katrina and the oil spill. During our trip, Gavin caught two stingrays, Garon caught two catfish, and I caught a foot-long fish, not sure what type. The most interesting aspect of the event, though, was chatting with our fishing guide, who told us that post-Katrina the area was finally coming back to life. While many people had left the area, many people stayed because of their love for the community.

I found this so inspiring and renewed my resolve that when we returned to the Los Angeles area, our family would do its part to make LA a great place to live. Where many people see obstacles, I want to see opportunities.

As we stepped off the fishing boat with our catch, I caught myself wondering how an extra man had climbed on board—then realized that I was looking at Garon. He was getting visibly taller by the day and outgrowing his clothes at a rapid pace. Since he'd turned thirteen, Garon had added something besides height to his changes: snoring! On some mornings, he was the only one who woke up feeling he'd had a good night's sleep.

On January 24, we drove to Louisiana—the Pelican State—and checked into the French Quarter RV Resort in New Orleans. We arrived in the Big Easy about a week before the Super Bowl and two weeks before Mardi Gras, and many activities, celebrations, and parades led up to these events.

While we were not into drinking or partying, we did want to explore this remarkable city—hardest hit during Hurricane Katrina—and celebrate the endurance of its outstanding citizens. While we managed to take a quick daytime trek through the French Quarter, including Bourbon Street—where we caught some beads during the Mardi Gras parades—we were more interested in visiting the city's Ninth Ward, which had suffered the worst devastation during the hurricane. We visited the Hurricane Katrina Memorial, a granite marker that lists the names of people who lost their lives, and drove through some of the city's most hard-hit areas, places with boarded-up homes and people living on the fringes. Gavin was especially moved by the homeless people, and that night he prayed for everyone he'd seen that day.

Since the weather was good, we decided to head north and visit Memphis, where we checked into the Graceland RV park, directly across the street from Graceland, Elvis Presley's home, where the rock star lived from 1957 until his death in 1977. The next day, we toured Graceland—a nearly fourteen-acre estate, complete with a white-columned mansion and a collection of Elvis's cars and airplanes. The boys had never heard of Elvis Presley, so that night we watched one of his films; we were all impressed with his talent, especially his voice. We added Elvis's gospel tunes to our playlist in the RV.

The following day, January 29, we entered Arkansas—the Land of Opportunity—and traveled to Little Rock. A few hours after we checked into a hotel, sirens started to blare and emergency warnings appeared on TV and on our phones. We soon learned that the sirens and messages indicated severe weather and possible tornadoes. We made a pact: no more RV campgrounds until we were out of the tornado zone. This trip had really opened our eyes about the difficult and scary weather conditions that much of the country endures. In Little Rock, we kept our shoes on most of the time in case we needed to run to safety.

Right here, I would like to salute those stalwart citizens of the United States of America who endure and have endured so many weather-related trials, especially tornados and hurricanes—two of the most frightening conditions imaginable.

The tornados didn't touch down in Little Rock but hit other areas of Arkansas. When we ventured outside, a calm-after-the-storm feeling was in the air: eerily still and a bit somber. Gavin prayed that no one was hurt in the tornados that touched down.

The mood carried over into our visit to the Little Rock Central High School National Historic Site, which commemorates nine brave African-American students who, in 1957, enrolled in the racially segregated Little Rock Central High School. While the governor of Arkansas barred their entry, President Eisenhower intervened, enabling the students to attend the school based on the 1954 Supreme Court ruling declaring segregated schools unconstitutional. We were inspired by the brave students who endured threats and violence to achieve their dreams of a sound education.

The following day, we added another presidential library to our list, visiting the William J. Clinton Presidential Center. The main building cantilevers over the Arkansas River, echoing Clinton's campaign promise of "building a bridge to the twenty-first century." Whatever your politics or opinion of Bill Clinton, you must admit that he has shown remarkable endurance.

On February 1, we entered Oklahoma—the Sooner State, so named for the settlers in the late eighteen hundreds that arrived "sooner" than expected to claim land in what was previously the Indian Territory. We checked into a hotel in Broken Arrow on the outskirts of Tulsa. Now that we'd hit Oklahoma, we felt as if we were in the West—maybe it only seemed as though everyone was wearing cowboy hats and boots, but it was pretty close.

The RV needed some work, so I arranged to leave it at a repair facility and pick up a rental to use for a few days.

Now that we were in shouting distance (well, if we yelled really loud) of home, Melinda was feeling wistful about the trip ending. She was finally getting into the swing of things, and the trip was almost over. I knew what she meant—I too was going to miss our time on the road.

At the Gilcrease Museum in Tulsa, we learned about Native American history, culture, and art in a beautiful setting. Afterward, we discussed what had occurred during the eighteen hundreds, when Native American tribes were moved to what is now Oklahoma, as their lands were taken over in other parts of the country. Somehow, these proud tribes have endured, despite all the hardships and injustices they have suffered.

On February 4, I picked up a rental car, and we drove to Bentonville, Arkansas, home of Walmart, our sometime home during the trip. We visited the original Walton's 5&10 Store, which opened on May 9, 1950, which also features a small museum filled with the owner's artifacts and memorabilia. We said a silent thank-you to Mr. Walton for his hospitality during our journey.

The same day, we headed for Joplin, Missouri, and stopped along the path where the massive tornado had hit on May 22, 2011. We stopped at Cunningham Park, which had been rebuilt to include a memorial to commemorate those who'd lost their lives in the tragedy. In the area, many homes had been rebuilt—a testament to the endurance of the residents—but many houses remained empty.

We headed north to Independence and visited the Harry S. Truman Library & Museum, which honors our thirty-third president. I'll admit I knew very little about Truman, other than that he'd assumed the presidency upon Franklin Roosevelt's death in 1945. I decided to add a Truman biography to my reading list.

George Arredondo

Now it was time to make up for an oversight; we'd missed Iowa (the Hawkeye State) when heading east, so we needed to make a northern detour while we were heading west. We reached Iowa at a colder time of year than we would have a few months before, but we still managed to have a great time. There was snow on the ground, and the boys had a great snowball slugfest. We drove past many farms, which Melinda loved because they looked so peaceful.

Highlights included visiting the picturesque bridges of Madison County (made famous in the book and movie of the same name), touring the birthplace of John Wayne in a tiny house that his father built, and stopping by the world's largest truck stop. We also toured the Herbert Hoover Presidential Library in West Branch, a site run by the National Park Service, which enabled Gavin to earn his junior-ranger badge.

After a few days in Iowa, we set off for Nebraska—the Cornhusker State—on a cold, rainy day. We traveled to Omaha and headed to Boys Town, a home for underprivileged and neglected boys founded by Father Edward Flanagan in 1917. While the home started out caring for five boys, today it hosts five hundred boys and girls in seventy homes. The site also includes schools, churches, medical facilities, a police station, and a museum. A statue on the site commemorates the boy who said, "He's not heavy. He's my brother."

While leaving Omaha the following day, we stopped along the Missouri River, which creates the border of Iowa and Nebraska. We viewed the historic area where Lewis and Clark stopped on their expedition during the early eighteen hundreds, when they were exploring the area known as the Louisiana Purchase for President Thomas Jefferson.

Our next stop was Kansas—the Sunflower State—and we traveled to a spot one mile north of Lebanon that represents the center of the forty-eight contiguous states. There was something truly awesome about standing on this spot—at thirty-nine degrees latitude and ninety-eight degrees longitude—in this quaint area in the middle of farmland. As Gavin said, "We are in the heartland of America."

While in Kansas, we visited the Dwight D. Eisenhower Presidential Library and Museum in Abilene, which honors our thirty-fourth president.

While there, Garon and Gavin earned the Boy Scout and Cub Scout Dwight D. Eisenhower Leadership Patch.

On February 14, as we were leaving Kansas, Gavin surprised Melinda with a Valentine's bag of goodies. She really enjoyed the beautiful cards with loving messages from the boys.

The same day we arrived in Oklahoma City, where we paid our respects at the Oklahoma City National Memorial and Museum, which honors all who were affected by the bombing of the Federal Building on April 19, 1995. This was a solemn occasion but another reason to celebrate the endurance of our citizens.

From Mobile, Gulfport, New Orleans, Joplin, and Oklahoma City, we learned so much about the American spirit, and we are forever grateful.

CHAPTER 14

Deep in the Heart

IN MANY WAYS, our trip across America had been about me getting back in touch with myself and understanding, on deeper levels, who I am, what I'm all about and what I value. The journey helped me not only get in touch with myself but also establish a closer and more meaningful relationship with my wife and sons.

Now that we were headed to Texas, the trip's significance as a journey into myself came to the fore because we were about to enter the state where I was born. I arrived on this earth in El Paso, Texas, the sixth of eight children born to Felix and Bertha Arredondo—both native Texans.

On February 18, we entered Texas—the Lone Star State—and checked into Loyd Park, a beautiful RV campground in Grand Prairie, about a half hour south of Dallas. Garon said the park was so secluded and deserted—only about twenty campers were in a site that could accommodate five hundred—that it was as if we had a nice, big backyard with our own lake. As soon as he jumped out of the RV, Garon headed for the water.

During the trip, we'd visited the birthplaces of presidents, authors, and movie stars, and now I was about to share the place of my nativity with Garon and Gavin. I felt as if I were completing something meaningful and significant. I wanted to share many aspects of Texas with my family—and in so doing, I was sharing various aspects of myself.

Our first excursion, a must do, was lunch in downtown Dallas at El Fenix, where Tex-Mex cuisine was born in 1918. We'd eaten at many Mexican restaurants during our trip—some excellent, some good, and some not so good—but nothing compared to the fare at El Fenix. Bravo!

Fifty States, Fifty Weeks

After lunch, we engaged in a serious and solemn activity: visiting Dealey Plaza, where President John F. Kennedy was shot and killed on November 22, 1963, about six months before I was born. As had other cities where tragedies had occurred, Dallas had created memorials to the fallen, including a museum to honor our thirty-fifth president.

During the trip, we had visited many places where tragic incidents had occurred, including the World Trade Center, the Federal Building in Oklahoma City, and the 16th Street First Baptist Church, and it was often difficult to explain the whats and whys of these events to my sons. Dealey Plaza was no different, but it felt more personal because this crime had taken place in my home state. All I could really say was, "Sometimes bad things happen in America, and we have to learn from these experiences so that good things will happen in America."

Loyd Park offered many opportunities for activities, such as running, walking, fishing, building campfires, and swimming (although it was still too cold for that). Since it was sparsely populated at this time of year, I couldn't help but think of adding another activity to the list: teaching Garon to drive. How better for my son to remember the state of Texas than to recall that he'd learned to drive there?

I hoped to make this a positive experience for Garon, unlike the driving lesson I'd endured with my father. When I was fifteen, I mentioned to my dad one Sunday morning that I was taking driver's ed at school. The next thing I knew, my dad told me we were going for a ride, but when we got outside, he directed me to get into the driver's seat of his Volkswagen Rabbit. I had mixed emotions. I was excited about driving but anxious about the car's manual clutch and gearshift.

In high school, we had not yet reached the point of driving—our studies had focused on the rules of the road. The first time I'd tried to drive a car was in my dad's VW, and I did drive it—for about ten feet, the worst ten feet in my life. During the twenty-minute lesson, my father badgered, berated, and bullied me to the point that he achieved his goal. After I completed driver's ed, I never asked to borrow his car.

However, I vowed that someday I would drive farther than anyone in my family had ever ventured. I promised myself that I'd eventually drive any type of vehicle, mastering cars and trucks, including those with manual transmissions. Here I was, driving through all fifty states. I wished my dad were still around to see it.

I promised myself that Garon's driving lesson would be a positive, memorable experience—one that he'd recall fondly for the rest of his life. However, Garon's driving lesson turned out to be more brief than the one I'd experienced with my father—and not because I was impatient or unhelpful.

When I asked Garon to get behind the wheel of our rental car for a driving lesson, he said, "I've been waiting for this." He was excited and couldn't wait to start driving around the roads in our campground. However, I told him first that I needed to explain the theory of driving. As I was lecturing on the finer points of offensive and defensive driving, Garon was having trouble keeping his eyes open. He let out a yawn—not to be rude but because he just couldn't help it.

"I know all this, Dad," he said.

"OK," I told him. "Start the engine and show me what you can do."

That was just what he did. I was amazed as Garon fired up the engine and took off down the road, driving with ease and confidence, his arm resting on the rolled-down window. He acted as if he'd been driving all his life. And why not? He'd had years of experience driving cars while playing video games!

After he practiced parking for a while, I told him to drive up to the RV and honk the horn. Gavin poked his head out the window and called to Melinda, saying, "Mom, Dad has lost it. Garon is driving."

When he got out of the car, Garon flipped me the keys and said, "Let me know when you need me to drive the RV." Well, he *had* served as co-pilot in forty-four states!

From that time on, whenever I got out of the RV at a gas station, Garon hopped into the driver's seat. When we attended a Monster Jam at Cowboys Stadium, I could tell that Garon was ready to jump in one of the monster trucks in case one of the drivers needed some help.

While in Dallas, we fulfilled one of Melinda's goals for the trip by attending church at The Potter's House with Reverend T. D. Jakes. The message, called "The Day Isn't Over," really hit home, expressing that we needed to keep fighting the good fight, and it left us feeling inspired and motivated.

A great day got even greater when we attended an NBA game at American Airlines Center and watched the Lakers beat the Mavericks, 103–109. We celebrated with dinner at Benihana, a Japanese restaurant where they prepare food on grills right in front of you. A real treat!

We left our idyllic surroundings in Grand Prairie and headed for Irving, about fifteen minutes north, and made one of our pilgrimage stops of the trip: the National Scouting Museum, the official museum of the Boy Scouts of America. I sometimes wish my childhood had included Scouting experiences, but I had to learn other sets of survival skills growing up in LA. Through my sons, I see the value of Scouting in building character and fitness and tip my hat to founder of the Scout movement, Robert Baden-Powell.

George Arredondo

After a few days in College Station, where the boys and I attended a Texas A&M baseball game and we visited the George Bush Presidential Library and Museum, honoring the forty-first president of the United States, we made our way to Houston. After a few days at bare-bones RV parks, we were ready to check into a hotel—thankful for hot showers and a basketball court for Gavin.

Our tour of Houston featured a visit to the San Jacinto battleground from Texas's war for independence, the site where Texas won its independence from Mexico on April 21, 1836. The twelve-hundred-acre site is home to the USS *Texas*, the San Jacinto Museum of History, and the San Jacinto Monument, which is a 567-foot monument that honors the people who fought for Texas's independence and is the world's tallest memorial stone column. I loved learning more about Texas's history; it made me feel as if I knew myself a bit better. My parents were proud Texans and imparted this pride to all their children.

Texas pride isn't complete without a visit to Minute Maid Park, home of the Houston Astros baseball team. Later, we ate at a Mexican restaurant, and Melinda told me that I can really find some great spots to eat. I try!

On Sunday, March 3, we were excited to attend worship services at Lakewood Church, the largest church in the United States, with Pastor Joel Osteen. What a wonderful church—and what a wonderful message! Osteen encouraged worshipers to find opportunities each day for acts of kindness. The boys really enjoyed the message and participating in the service with over forty thousand people!

In many ways, the entire trip had been like a church service in that we were joining with millions of other Americans to celebrate the wonders of God's creation and honor the history of our great nation. Hallelujah!

The following day, we had a family field trip—with a reprieve from classwork for the boys—to Space Center Houston, the official visitors' center at NASA's Johnson Space Center. The boys really enjoyed the experience, especially our visit to mission control, where the ground-support team monitors and directs flights from seconds after launch through landing. During the trip, we had so many great opportunities to learn about the space program and space travel. I thought of the Apollo 13 mission in 1970—"Houston, we have a problem"—and the heroic crews in the air and on the ground who brought the ship home after an oxygen tank exploded, damaging the vessel. The American spirit at its best!

On March 5, we arrived at a KOA campground in San Antonio and realized the spring-vacation season must have started, judging by the high number of RVs at the site. I loved the location because the San Antonio Country Club's golf course was right around the corner, and I managed to tee off a few times. The location was special because Lee Trevino had won the San Antonio Texas Open at that course in 1980, and I struck up a conversation with a member who gave me a first-person account of Trevino's win. That day, I not only played golf; I also got a history lesson.

George Arredondo

March 6 is a special day in San Antonio: the anniversary of the Battle of the Alamo in 1836, when Texas's forces were wiped out by the Mexican Army. Before his death, Lieutenant Colonel William B. Travis, commander of the Texan rebels, wrote a letter pleading for help and signing it "Victory or Death." The letter inspired volunteers to join the rebels, resulting in victory at San Jacinto, the site we'd visited the previous week in Houston. We stood in line for nearly two hours to view this historic artifact. There was just so much about Texas to learn—it was a big state with a big history.

On March 11, we headed toward the Texas capital, Austin, picking up Melinda's brother Nick in nearby San Marcos. Melinda couldn't get over how much her younger brother resembled her dad. We really enjoyed Nick's company as we made our way around Austin, with stops that included lunch at a great burger joint called Huts and a visit to the Lyndon B. Johnson Presidential Library, which honors our thirty-sixth president.

While it seemed that we were showing Nick around his home turf, he turned the tables on us at the Texas State Capitol, which was closed for tours. As we stood outside, Nick spotted one of his friends leaving the building, and we were able to get behind the ropes for a personal tour. As we were about to enter the building, Rick Perry (governor at the time) walked out, looked right at me, and said, "Hello. How you doing?" Wow, the native son returns and is greeted by none other than the governor of Texas. What are the odds of that? It was especially at moments like these that I saw the hand of God in our trip.

After a week in San Antonio, we drove to Sonora, Texas, where we settled down at the Caverns of Sonora RV park, surrounded by cactus. We were in the real West! The weather during the day hit eighty, and it felt really, really good. While here, we walked the two miles through the Caverns of Sonora, which are considered some of the most beautiful caves in the world.

Our tour through the caverns put me into an introspective mood. As I listened to the tour guide explain how the caves were discovered when someone watched a dog chase a raccoon into an opening in the rock, I thought about all the places in ourselves that we don't pay attention to until something happens to make us notice. Since quitting my job and embarking on the trip, I had been getting to know myself a bit more each day.

On March 14, we arrived at what became Melinda's favorite spot on the trip: the X Bar Ranch, a working ranch in the Texas Hill Country, run for over a century by the Meador family. We stayed at the Round House, a circular rock house located on the edge of a hill in the center of the ranch. All around us was nature, nature, and more nature; birds, sheep, cattle, goats, and deer; plus beautiful surroundings and ideal weather.

After a spectacular few days at the X Bar Ranch, where Melinda and the boys hope to return someday, we took off for our final Texas destination: my birthplace, El Paso.

On March 17, we spent the day with my Uncle Pete and Aunt Anna and their family. Uncle Pete, my father's younger brother, told us many stories about his brother Felix. He said that my father was adventurous, joining the navy at age seventeen and moving to California when he returned from the service. He said my dad was always looking for a chance to learn something new. "You're a lot like Felix," Uncle Pete told me.

It felt so good to get in touch with my extended family and my roots, including my cousin Julie and her sons, and learn more about my father. It made me feel closer to him and remember his great qualities: his intelligence, humor, diligence, endurance, and determination—components of the American spirit that I'd learned about during the trip.

I was so glad for the month in Texas where I could share my native state with my sons and show them what the Lone Star State had to offer. As we were preparing to leave, Garon told me, "I'd move to Texas." Mission accomplished.

George Arredondo

CHAPTER 15

Heading Home

As we made the turn and headed west out of Texas, it hit all of us that we were in the homestretch—the last thousand miles and final thirty days of our journey. Melinda, the boys, and I all had mixed feelings; we were sorry to see this once-in-a-lifetime experience end but excited about the future and our new life in Southern California.

Growing up listening to Vin Scully provide play-by-play for the Dodgers games on the radio, I developed a real sense of wanderlust, listening to the announcer's descriptions of cities on the road. I made a pact with myself to visit these places someday, and now I had fulfilled that dream. However, when one dream is completed, a new one takes hold—and that's why I'm writing this book: I want to share what I've learned on my journey, and I learned so much during our final days on the road.

After an overnight stay at an RV park in Lordsburg, New Mexico, on March 19, we headed for Arizona. Our goal was to reach Tucson a few days later to attend some MLB spring-training games (Gavin was counting on it!).

We definitely felt we were in the Southwest—Melinda especially loved the desert landscape—and enjoyed the sights as we drove to Arizona, the Grand Canyon State. Our first stop was an Old West town called Tombstone, which was so authentic that it felt as if we'd stepped into the late eighteen hundreds. Founded in 1877, the town thrived, thanks to the gold and silver mines in the area, and became a magnet for outlaws and lawmen.

Today, Tombstone survives mainly as a tourist attraction and features actors reenacting the Old West days, including the infamous gunfight at the OK Corral, fought between a gang of outlaws and a group of lawmen, including Wyatt Earp.

Garon and Gavin got a big kick out of this live theater performance, and as I watched the action, I thought about all the history we'd viewed on the trip—from the earliest settlers at Jamestown, through colonial times, through the Revolutionary War, through the Civil War, and now the Old West. This was such an amazing country, and I never ceased to be amazed at our remarkable history.

If there is one message I want to communicate in this book, it's this: Explore the great land that is America, find out about our rich history, and learn about the heroic people who came before us. You don't have to quit your job and hit the road for fifty weeks, but you can spend weekends exploring places close to your home or vacations checking out somewhere you've never been before. Remember, the world starts at your driveway—you can go anywhere from there.

From Tombstone, we made our way to Tucson and then took a day-trip to Saguaro National Park, a site that includes nearly a hundred thousand acres in the Sonoran Desert. The area is renowned for its vast acreage of saguaro cacti, the giant plants made famous in Western movies. We had a great time hiking and exploring in this magnificent location.

On the first day of spring, we were in Tucson, attending a Dodgers/Cubs spring-training game at Kino Stadium. The boys were ecstatic that the Dodgers won in a close five-to-four game. I could almost hear Vin Scully narrating the victory. After the game, we traveled to Apache Junction, where we checked into a KOA campground packed with people on spring break.

The following day, I took Gavin to see the Angels play the Royals in Phoenix, and Gavin was in his element, watching his favorite player, Albert Pujols. While in Phoenix, we also had the chance to visit with cousins from my mom's side of the family, who treated us to a barbecue and plenty of hospitality as we told stories about our trip. I was so happy to reconnect with family members during our travels—nothing is more important than faith and family.

On our way to spring training in Scottsdale, we stopped at the quaint town of Tortilla Flat, located in the middle of the Tonto National Forest in the Superstition Mountains, and then continued on the Apache Trail Historic Road. Everywhere we looked, the scenery was breathtaking.

The boys were still busy with schoolwork as we traveled from place to place, and Melinda said they would finish in mid-June. We were both happy with the way homeschooling had turned out for our sons; and all the time on the road had been one huge learning experience.

After checking into a Scottsdale resort, we headed out for a Dodgers spring-training game at Camelback Ranch-Glendale, where our team beat the White Sox. Go Dodger Blue! We'd brought our players luck so far!

George Arredondo

Scottsdale weather was a perfect eighty degrees, and we all felt good in the T-shirt temperatures. It was great to see Melinda get some pampering at the spa, since she'd been working so hard, taking care of business matters, preparing taxes, and managing everything related to the boys' schoolwork. While at the resort, Garon, Gavin, and I had fun hitting golf balls at the batting cages.

We were looking forward to one of the major events of the trip: an excursion to the Grand Canyon. After driving to the Grand Canyon RV park in Williams, Arizona, where, at an elevation of seven thousand feet, it was at least twenty degrees colder than it was in Scottsdale, we tried to get a good night's sleep to make sure we were well rested and ready to explore the Grand Canyon.

The next morning, we made our way to the Grand Canyon Railway Depot, where we hopped aboard a train that carried us on a two-hour ride to the Grand Canyon—and the scenery was spectacular the entire way. After lunch, we took a bus tour that made stops at various spots on the canyon's rim. Later, we checked into Maswik Lodge and spent a quiet evening strolling through the area and enjoying the magnificent night sky, which featured more stars than I'd ever seen.

For Melinda and me, it was our second trip to the Grand Canyon. During our first visit, she was pregnant with Garon, so in a sense, it was his second visit too. What a great way to spend the final days of our trip—in an awe-inspiring, majestic setting that is truly one of the seven natural wonders of the world. At two hundred and seventy-seven miles long, eighteen miles wide, and six thousand feet deep, nearly two billion years of our planet's history were exposed when the Colorado River and its tributaries cut channels through layer after layer of rock and created the Grand Canyon.

While many tourists stick to bus tours when visiting the Grand Canyon, just getting out for a few minutes to say they've seen it, we explored the area for two days, including taking a three-mile hike along the rim. Garon stood on a rock and declared himself king of the world. A trip highlight occurred for Gavin while we were there: we found a restaurant that served some of the best mac and cheese of the trip.

Fifty States, Fifty Weeks

Here's something else I learned on the journey: It's better to explore one place in depth than to just skim the surface of several places. Spend time learning about a location, meditating about it, letting it sink into your soul. You'll get much more out of your travels if you slow down and focus on one site at a time.

After our trip to the Grand Canyon, we picked up our RV in Williams and headed back to New Mexico—the Land of Enchantment—where we visited Meteor Crater, the imprint that remained when a meteor collided with Earth fifty thousand years ago, leaving a crater a mile across and over five hundred feet deep.

First the Grand Canyon and then the Meteor Crater—wide-open spaces that made me think of the future and how I was starting over in a new area, a new line of work, and with a new set of priorities: faith and family first. Spring was in the air, and it felt good to realize I was experiencing a new beginning. I decided to map out my lifeline, listing everything that had happened in my life, the highs and the lows, with a goal of understanding the lows and fully living the highs.

After staying overnight at the historic El Ranch Hotel in Gallup, New Mexico, we fulfilled one of Melinda's goals for the trip and headed to Santa Fe, the oldest capital city in the United States, dating back to 1610. Melinda really enjoyed exploring this quintessentially Southwestern city, with its adobe architecture and ancient Spanish-style churches. She said the town turned out just as she imagined it would be and told us she was in love with Santa Fe. I was so glad we made a detour so she could experience this great place.

On Easter Sunday, March 31, we entered Colorado—the Centennial State, so named because its statehood occurred in 1876, a hundred years after the Declaration of Independence. We had reached our forty-seventh state. Our first stop was Durango, established as a railroad hub in the late eighteen hundreds. While touring the historic downtown area, we discovered a tiny museum with a fascinating collection of baseball memorabilia and artifacts—an homage to the family's deceased patriarch, a dedicated collector. It always warmed my heart when I learned about loving relationships between fathers and children. To me, this was one of life's main purposes.

We left the baseball-memorabilia museum in time to see the real thing on TV: the Dodgers' opening game against the Giants. Our team was off to a flying start! Go Dodgers!

The next day, we drove through the beautiful, snowy San Juan Mountains to Silverton, where gold was discovered in 1860. I understood the gold-rush mentality, leaving everything to pursue a dream. I'd pretty much done the same thing—not for worldly treasure but for the treasures of faith and family.

The drive down the San Juan Mountains was spectacular, with breathtaking views. We pulled over to take photos of the falling snow, and Gavin and I even got in a game of catch amid the flakes.

On April 4, we drove to Mesa Verde National Park in Montezuma County, Colorado, near the Four Corners (where Utah, Colorado, Arizona, and New Mexico meet). President Theodore Roosevelt created the park in 1906 to preserve cliff dwellings of the Ancestral Puebloan people. Our drive up to the site's museum and the preserved dwellings gave us astounding views for over twenty miles of winding roads at an altitude of seventy-five hundred feet. We met a park ranger who was fascinated by our traveling tales and told us it had always been her dream to visit all fifty states. She couldn't seem to get enough of our stories and even asked the boys to show her our route on the map.

As she was about to offer a remark, Gavin beat her to the punch, saying, "Go ahead; say it."

She smiled and told him, "You're so lucky."

It was at least the hundredth time we'd heard this, but we never got tired of the words. Yes, we were lucky—very, very lucky.

The ranger ended up giving us the royal tour of the sites, and we felt as if we had struck gold in terms of beauty, history, and culture.

The next day was filled with dramatic scenery and dramatic moments as we stood on the Four Corners National Monument and later drove to the otherworldly Monument Valley Navajo Tribal Park. Research revealed that RVs measuring twenty-five feet or over were not recommended for the seventeen-mile unpaved dirt road down into the valley, but I made a calculated decision to take the drive. We were rewarded with incredible views of the buttes, mesas, canyons, and freestanding rock formations. In some ways, I felt as if I were back at the beginning of time, witnessing the creation of the world.

Each place we visited during this leg of the trip seemed to wow us even more. We had a great time at Lake Powell, the world's largest manmade lake at the Arizona/Utah border, where the boys and I caught striped bass and, along with Melinda, enjoyed a fabulous boat tour.

Then we hit Zion National Park in Utah—the Beehive State, our forty-eighth state—and couldn't believe we'd never made our way to this location during previous vacations. As Melinda wrote on our blog that night, "Zion National Park, set in the southwest corner of Utah, is a masterpiece of cliffs, deep red canyons, mesas, and buttes." *Masterpiece* is definitely the word for this awe-inspiring location.

While in Utah, we had to visit my namesake town, Saint George. I'd always loved the story about Saint George slaying the dragon, and I felt that the trip had helped me slay a variety of dragons, including personal insecurity and negative stress.

George Arredondo

On April 11, we arrived in state forty-nine: Nevada, the Silver State. We were really counting down now. Just eleven more days and we'd hop on a plane to Hawaii, our final destination.

After a few days in Las Vegas, we made our way to the Hoover Dam, named for our thirty-first president, Herbert Hoover. It was remarkable to witness how the dam harnessed the power of the mighty Colorado River—a stunning feat of engineering that was accomplished because of the people who dreamed it and then saw the project through to completion. Built during the Great Depression, from 1931–1936, the Hoover Dam is a feat of American ingenuity and sacrifice, an effort that required thousands of workers, the dangerous work costing over a hundred lives.

On April 15, we left Nevada and headed toward home, taking a nice, easy drive, starting at about ten in the morning and arriving at four in the afternoon. We knew we were home when we encountered Southern California traffic!

For the next week, we focused on getting acclimated to our new environment, meeting with friends and family, eating at our favorite Mexican restaurants, and enrolling the kids in school, as well as preparing our home and storing the RV. It was a busy week, and we were ready for our island getaway to conclude our travels.

We took an 8:00 a.m. flight to Honolulu on April 22, and a few hours later, we entered state fifty. We let out a cheer—we had achieved our goal! Beforehand, we'd agreed that this would be a real vacation—no history lessons, studying, books, or homeschooling—just fun and relaxation.

At our hotel, I overheard some college umpires talking about a local baseball game between California State, Fullerton (Melinda's alma mater), and the University of Hawaii. When I explained that I officiated at college-level sports, they said they'd leave tickets for us at the stadium. Go Titans!

Another treat was eating at Gavin's favorite Burger King—we'd taken the boys to Hawaii on a previous vacation—below the Marriott Hotel. We were all in bliss as we chowed down on the burgers in the final state on our journey.

We checked into a hotel near Waikiki Beach—deciding to stay on Oahu for the entire ten days—and took in the island's many delights, including visiting the Dole Plantation, Diamond Head, and the Atlantis Submarines and attending the Magic of Polynesia magic show.

One of our favorite spots was Iolani Palace, the restored residence of the Kalākaua dynasty that ruled the Kingdom of Hawaii from 1874–1893. Yes, America once had a king—King Kalākaua, who reigned for seventeen years in the eighteen hundreds. As I stood there, I felt like a king, too. Well, more like a president, having traveled to all fifty states in this great nation in fifty weeks. Only four presidents have, while in office for more than four years, traveled to all fifty states. None of my favorite leaders of all time—George Washington, Abraham Lincoln, and John F. Kennedy—would travel to all our states. I had traveled to all fifty states and had experienced the amazing treasures that America has to offer with the most important persons in my life.

At Pu'u Ualaka State Park, Gavin brought along an American Flag for a picture of the occasion. Fifty states in fifty weeks was a reality—and an adventure we'd never forget. Like the kings of our past, we had reached the mountain top!

Afterword

As I reflect back on one of the greatest years in my life, I am reminded of a quote by Mark Twain: **"The two most important days of your life, the day you were born and the day you find out why."** I now live more freely than ever and with less concern for myself. I have discovered the *why* of my life. Each of us lives for a very short period in the world, and our past transgressions and fears of the future can grip much of our living. When you spend time living in the present with the ones you love most, it changes you and allows you the freedom to experience life more fully.

I have been inspired to write this book and share the experience of fifty states in fifty weeks with others who may one day dream bigger and live fuller! Travel America, and you'll find it is a great place to find your why. Fifty States in Fifty Weeks can start from any driveway, in any city across America.

It all started with one question: "If I had one year to live, how would I live it?"

Made in the USA
Middletown, DE
06 November 2023